Key Stage 3

Revision Notes

*S*cience

Levels 4–7

Authors
John Collinson
John Dobson
Janet Granycome

Series editor
Alan Brewerton

EDUCATIONAL

Every effort has been made to trace copyright holders and to obtain their permission for the use of copyright material. The authors and publishers will gladly receive information enabling them to rectify any error or omission in subsequent editions.

First published 1998
1999 Edition first published 1998

Letts Educational, Schools and Colleges Division, 9–15 Aldine Street, London W12 8AW
Tel. 0181 740 2270
Fax 0181 740 2280

Text © John Collinson, John Dobson, Janet Granycome 1998

Editorial, design and production by Hart McLeod, Cambridge

British Library Cataloguing-in-Publication Data
A CIP record for this book is available from the British Library

ISBN 1 84085 138 4

Printed and bound in Great Britain

Letts Educational is the trading name of BPP (Letts Educational) Ltd

Acknowledgements
The authors and publishers are grateful to the staff at Cottenham Village College, Cambridge and St. David's School, Middlesbrough for their technical assistance with this project.

Contents

Life processes and living things

Materials and their properties

Physical processes

Preparing for your Key Stage 3 SATs

You may remember taking National Tests (often called SATs) in Science, English and Maths when you were about 7 and 11 years old. Your Key Stage 3 SATs, taken in May at the end of Year 9, are the last National Tests that you will take before your GCSE examinations in two years' time.

The Key Stage 3 SATs are important because they help show how much you have improved in these three important subjects. They will also help you, your parents and your teachers plan ahead for your GCSE courses next year. Your teachers may use the results of your SATs to help place you in the most appropriate teaching group for some of your GCSE courses.

It is, therefore, a good idea to be well prepared when you take your SATs. Good preparation will lead to good marks and increased confidence. This is where this book is of value.

How to use this book

This book will help you prepare for your SATs in the easiest possible way. It is clearly divided into National Curriculum topics which you will have covered during the past three years. The information is presented as a series of facts, explanations and examples which will help to refresh your memory and improve your understanding.

The book also contains useful tips and advice from examiners which show you how to avoid common mistakes and improve your marks. There is also space for you to make your own notes and comments. Each section finishes with a short test so that you can check that you have covered the topic sufficiently.

Your SATs are important, and this book gives you an excellent opportunity of making the most of them.

Good luck

Life processes and living things

Characteristics of living things

Biology is the science of living things.

To be considered as living, *all* of the following seven characteristics must be present. Some non-living things have some characteristics but never all seven.

- **Movement** – all living things can move. Animals move their whole bodies. Plants can move parts of their bodies – e.g. leaves turn towards the sun, flowers can open and close – some leaves move when touched.

- **Respiration** – is the release of energy from food. It is essential to all life. Respiration happens in all living cells. Plants and animals use oxygen to release energy from food.

- **Sensitivity** – living things can sense and respond to changes in the environment. Animals respond quickly by moving. Plants usually respond slowly by growing.

- **Feeding** – all living things need food. It provides energy and other essential substances – e.g. proteins for growth, carbohydrates for energy. Animals feed on other living things. Plants make their food using energy from light.

- **Excretion** – is the removal from the body of waste products such as urea, carbon dioxide and water.

- **Reproduction** – all living things produce young. Plants and animals reproduce to make sure their species continues after they die.

- **Growth** – all living things get bigger. Animals grow until they become adult. Some plants never stop growing.

Remember these by the phrase MRS FERG:
Movement
Respiration
Sensitivity
Feeding
Excretion
Reproduction
Growth.

Note – Excretion is **not** the removal of the waste from digestion. This is called egestion or elimination.

Cells

All living things are made up of cells.

Each living thing may be made up of millions of cells like humans or trees. Some living things only have one cell like the simple animal called amoeba.

All animal cells have three basic parts:

It is very important to learn the names of the parts of plant and animal cells.

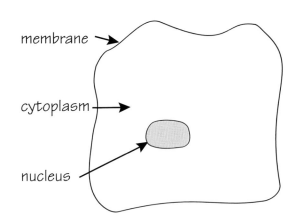

- **Cell membrane** – the outside wall of the cell. It allows certain chemicals to move in and out of the cell.

- **Cytoplasm** – this contains many tiny structures which keep a cell alive.

- **Nucleus** – the control centre of a cell. This contains the information needed to make a living thing.

Plant cells

Plant cells contain all the features of animal cells, but can have some extra ones:

- **Cellulose cell wall** – gives the plant cell strength and makes it tough and rigid.

- **Vacuole** – is a space filled with water. When it is full of water the plant cell is strong and rigid. The cell is said to be **turgid**.

- **Chloroplasts** – contain green **chlorophyll**. Chlorophyll absorbs light. The plant uses light energy to make food and grow.

- **Cell membrane** – allows certain chemicals to move in and out of the cell. It is just inside the cellulose cell wall.

- **Cytoplasm** – contains many tiny structures which keep a cell alive. Some structures inside the cytoplasm are **chloroplasts** and the **nucleus**.

- **Nucleus** – the control centre of a cell. This contains the information needed to make a living thing.

Test yourself! Can you draw and label the cells without looking? – **this is important!**

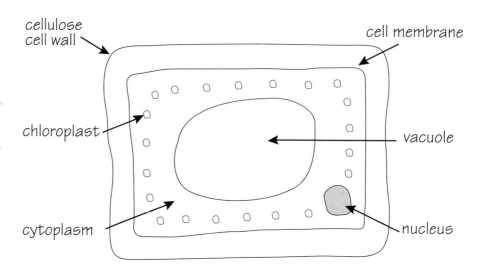

Cells, tissues, organs and systems

Most living things have many different parts – e.g. animals have muscle and blood. Plants have seeds, leaves, etc.
The cells of these different parts have features that make them specialised to do certain jobs. Cells can group together to form:

- **Tissues** – are specialised groups of identical cells.
  They all have the same job.

- **Organs** – many tissues grouped together for one job make up an organ.

- **System** – many organs grouped together for a specific job make up a system.

- **Organisms** – all the systems grouped together form an organism.

Examples

Try to learn the names of some cells, organs and systems.

- **Muscle tissue** – contains lots of identical muscle cells.
  Lung – organ containing the tissues – muscle + blood + nerve + other tissues.
  Respiratory system – contains the organs – lung + trachea + diaphragm + ribs + muscles.

- **Glandular tissue** – collection of glandular cells (producing enzymes, etc).
  Stomach – organ containing the tissues – glandular + nerve + muscle + blood + other tissues.
  Digestive system – system which includes – mouth + oesophagus + stomach + intestines + other organs.

- **Xylem tissue** – lots of xylem cells (they transport water in plants).
  Leaf – organ which contains the tissues – xylem + phloem + mesophyll + epidermis.

Types of cells

- **Sperm cell** – is the smallest cell in the body – it is designed to swim. It has a tail. The head contains the genes for the next generation. It also has an energy supply so it can swim a long way.

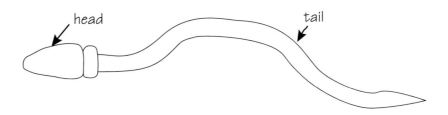

- **Muscle cell** – these cells can contract. They all fit together and if one cell contracts it makes all the others contract. Muscle tissue is found in all organs.

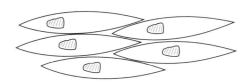

- **Ciliated epithelium** – are very specialised cells. They line the bronchioles, bronchi and trachea. The 'hair-like' structures are called cilia. The cilia move backwards and forwards and remove **mucus**, which traps dirt and germs, from the lungs. They keep the lungs clean. Cilia are damaged by smoking.

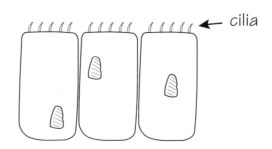
← cilia

Cell division

All cells (except human red blood cells) have **nuclei**.
Nuclei contain:

- **Chromosomes** – contain hundreds of **genes**. Think of the chromosome as being a string of beads, each bead representing one gene.

- **Genes** – control all the features of all living things.

Living things have pairs of chromosomes – e.g. each human cell has 23 pairs of chromosomes. This means there are 46 chromosomes in every nucleus of every cell in the body, except the sex cells.

For every characteristic there is a pair of genes – e.g. a pair of genes controls your eye colour, another pair your height.

Different genes for the same characteristic are called alleles. The genes in a pair do not have to be the same – your genes for eye colour may be one brown gene and one blue gene – but your eyes would be brown.

New cells are produced by the process of **cell division.**

Cell division is needed for the following:

- To grow until the living thing reaches maturity.

- To replace normal cells – e.g. red blood cells only live 120 days – they are always being replaced. Skin cells are also always being replaced. The cells that line your intestines are replaced every 2 or 3 days.

- To replace cells damaged by injury — e.g. broken bones or cuts and grazes.

- To make sex cells — sperm or ova in humans.

Transport across membranes

Chemicals move across cell membranes by the process of **diffusion**.
Diffusion is the movement of a substance from an area of high concentration to any area of low concentration. In living things it is usually through a semi-permeable membrane.

- Oxygen **diffuses** into the blood in the alveoli in the lungs — see respiration notes (page 18).

- Carbon dioxide **diffuses** into the air in the alveoli in the lungs.

- Carbon dioxide **diffuses** into leaves through stomata — see green plants notes (page 28).

- Small food molecules **diffuse** into the blood in the ileum — see digestive system notes (page 14).

The greater the concentration difference — the faster diffusion occurs.

Life processes and cell activity

Questions

1   What is 'responding to changes in the environment' called?

_____

2   What is the 'release of energy from food' called? _____

3   What is 'removing waste products from the body' called?

_____

4   What is 'producing new members of the species' called? _____

5   What is 'increasing in size' called? _____

6   Do animals or plants respond more quickly to a stimulus?

_____

7   Name the seven characteristics of living things.?

_____

_____

_____

_____

8   What are the inside contents of a cell called? _____

9   Which part of a cell controls its functions? _____

10 What is the outside of a plant cell called?_____

11 In which part of the plant cell is chlorophyll found? _____

12 Which part of the plant cell is filled with water? _____

13 What is a group of cells which have the same function called?

_____

14 What is a group of tissues which have one function called?

_____

15 What is a group of organs which have one function called?

_____

16 What do a group of organ systems make up? _____

17 Which features do animal cells not have?

_____

18 What is a neuron an example of?_____

19 What is the heart an example of? _____

20 What is the stomach an example of? _____

Humans as organisms

Diet

Humans need seven types of food in their diet (often called nutrition):

- **Carbohydrates** – are needed for **energy**. They are found in cereals, fruit and vegetables. Names of common **carbohydrates** are: starch, glucose, sugar (sucrose) and glycogen.

- **Proteins** – are made from **amino acids** and are used for growth and repair of cells. **Proteins** are found in meat, fish, eggs and beans.

- **Fats** – are made from fatty acids and glycerol. They are used for **energy** and to make **cell membranes**. Fats are found in milk, butter, cheese and margarine.

- **Minerals** – include iron for red blood cells and calcium for bones and teeth.

- **Vitamins** – include vitamins C and D.

- **Water** – dissolves soluble chemicals in the body.

- **Fibre** – this is roughage – it helps food travel along the digestive system.

Food tests

- **Glucose test** – add blue **Benedicts** to food solution and heat. Red/orange/yellow/green colour mean glucose is present.
  Red = lots of glucose,
  Green = very little glucose

- **Starch test** – add iodine to food solution. Blue-black means starch is present.

- **Protein test** (called Biuret) – add **Biuret** reagent to food plus sodium hydroxide. A purple colour means protein is present.

Digestion

- Large carbohydrates (starch), protein and fat are insoluble.

- Digestion breaks down large, insoluble, complex molecules into smaller, simpler, soluble molecules.

- Enzymes carry out digestion – they speed up chemical changes. They are catalysts.

Digestive system

Mouth

- Chewing food – breaks it into small pieces – makes it easier to swallow.

Saliva

Labelling diagrams, without looking at your notes, is a good way of learning the names of parts of the body.

- Starts to digest carbohydrate.

- Lubricates food.

- Makes food easier to swallow.

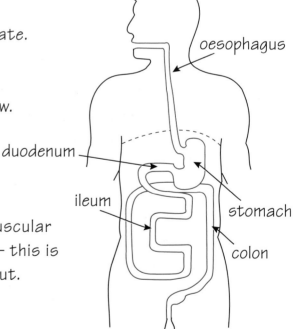

Oesophagus

- Gullet – food squeezed – muscular contractions – **peristalsis** – this is how food moves inside the gut.

Stomach

- **Hydrochloric acid** kills germs.

- Creates best conditions for enzyme.

- Enzyme digests protein.

Duodenum

Digestive juice from **pancreas**:

- Neutralises acid from stomach.

- Enzymes like slightly alkaline conditions.

- Enzymes digest all foods.

Bile

- Is made in the liver.

- It breaks fat up into tiny droplets to make digestion of fat easier – called emulsifying.

Note – Remember the names of the organs of the digestive system with the word MOSDICRA: **M**outh – **O**esophagus – **S**tomach – **D**uodenum – **I**leum – **C**olon – **R**ectum – **A**nus.

Ileum

- Enzymes complete digestion.

- Soluble, simple food is absorbed into bloodstream.

- Adapted for diffusion of small molecules – large surface area – **villi**.

- Thin, moist, semi-permeable cell membranes allow diffusion of food into blood.

- Active transport – for some molecules – energy used by cells to absorb food molecules.

Note – duodenum + ileum = small intestine.

Large intestine – colon

- Water is reabsorbed into blood – important as prevents dehydration.

- Indigestible food remains – **faeces**.

Rectum

- Stores faeces until they are eliminated or egested through **anus**.

Circulation

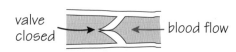
Remember –
A = Artery = Away

Blood vessels

Arteries

- Thick walls – elastic – have muscle.
- Need to withstand high pressure.
- Carry blood **away** from the heart.
- Deep in the body for protection.

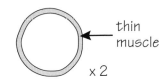
muscle

Artery (cross section)

Veins

- Thinner walls than arteries.
- Have **valves** to keep blood flowing towards the heart.
- Near muscles to help squeeze blood back to the heart.

valve closed — blood flow

Vein (longitudinal section)

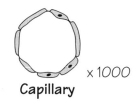
thin muscle
x 2

Vein (cross section)

Capillaries

- Very thin – walls one cell thick.
- Exchange food, oxygen, carbon dioxide, waste, cell products – between blood and organs.
- Capillary exchange mechanisms exist in all organs – e.g. ileum – villi, lung – alveoli, kidney – nephron.
- Provide very large surface area for diffusion.

x 1000
Capillary

Blood

Contains **red cells, white cells, platelets** and **plasma**.

Red Cells

- Carry **oxygen** in **haemoglobin**.
- Oxygen + haemoglobin ————> oxyhaemoglobin – in lungs.
- Oxyhaemoglobin ————> oxygen + haemoglobin – in all body cells.
- No nucleus – more room to carry oxygen.
- Made in bone marrow – live approximately 120 days.
- Poisoned by **carbon monoxide** – person suffocates from lack of oxygen.

membrane

red blood cell

White Cells

- Have nuclei.

- Made in bone marrow.

- **Immunity** – defend the body against any invaders – microbes such as bacteria, viruses.

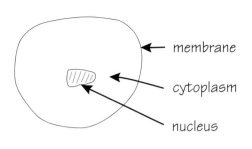

- Detect invaders and ingest (eat) them.

- **Antibodies** – made by white cells in lymph glands – destroy microbes and foreign tissue.

- **Antitoxins** – destroy poisons produced by microbes.

- **Immune system memory** – once you have had a disease you are usually immune – vaccinations trigger immune memory – boosters needed as a reminder for some diseases.

Note – you get lots of colds because the virus is different each time.

Platelets

- Made in bone marrow – from parts of much larger cells.

- React to cell damage/air.

- Produce fibres to trap red blood cells and **clot the blood**.

Plasma

- Liquid part of blood.

- Carries all cells.

- Dissolves **carbon dioxide** – carries it to lungs.

- Carries dissolved **food** from small intestine to liver and all cells.

- Carries **urea** from liver to kidneys.

Circulation of the blood

- The **heart** pumps blood to the **lungs**.

- The lungs **oxygenate** the blood.

- Blood returns to the **heart**.

- The heart pumps the blood around the **body**.

- **Arteries take blood away from the heart** to the liver, lungs, kidneys and other organs.

- **Veins take blood** from these organs **back to** the heart.

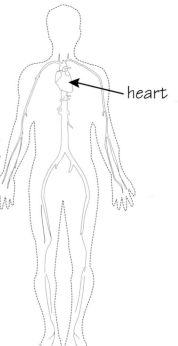

heart

Diseases

These are caused by **microbes** that invade the body. Microbe growth causes disease in different ways:

- Microbes produce toxins — poisons — when they grow.

- Microbes growing inside cells can cause cell death.

- Disease is made much worse by a person being weak — e.g. in the disease AIDS.

- A lot of microbes are usually needed to cause disease — unhygienic conditions — e.g. food poisoning (bacteria) or contact with infection — e.g. chicken pox (virus).

- See white blood cells (defence mechanisms, page 17).

Respiration

Breathing

The purpose of breathing is to:

- Take oxygen out of the air and put it into the blood.

- To take carbon dioxide out of the blood and put it back into the air.

Learn the position of ribs, trachea or windpipe, heart, diaphragm and lungs.

The structures concerned with breathing are:

- Ribs and muscles – to breathe in and out.

- Diaphragm – to breathe in and out.

- Trachea – connects the **lungs** to the air.

The lungs and chest cavity

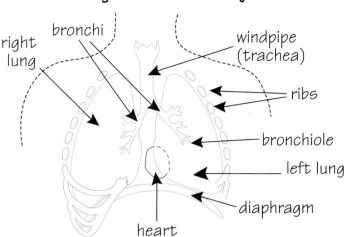

Lungs contain:

- Bronchi and bronchioles – the tubes that carry the air.

- Alveoli – where oxygen enters the blood from the air and carbon dioxide leaves the blood and enters the air.

Internal respiration is the production of energy within cells.

Aerobic respiration

Learn this equation!

GLUCOSE + OXYGEN ⟶ CARBON DIOXIDE + WATER + ENERGY

- Glucose is carried in blood plasma.

- Oxygen is carried in red blood cells.

- Cell cytoplasm – contains enzymes for respiration.

- Carbon dioxide is carried away by blood plasma.

Energy is used:

- To make molecules in cells – e.g. proteins from amino acids.

- Muscle contraction needs energy.

- Energy is given off as heat by birds and mammals to keep their bodies warm. They are warm blooded, which means that they have a constant body temperature.

Bones and skeleton

Skeleton is made of bones and has three functions:

- Protects parts of the body – e.g. skull – brain.

- Supports muscles for movement – e.g. arm.

- Makes blood cells.

Arm

- Biceps muscle contracts and raises the arm.

- Triceps muscle contracts and lowers the arm.

- Muscles work with and/or against each other – antagonistic.

- Muscles can only **pull** bones, not **push**.

biceps

triceps

upper arm bone

Nervous system

This detects changes in the environment. Humans can react to these changes. Nerves also co-ordinate animal behaviour.

Receptors

These detect the changes in the environment and they include:

- **Light** sensors in the **eye**.

- **Sound** sensors in the **ear**.

- **Balance** sensors which are also in the **ear**.

- **Taste** sensors on the **tongue**.

- **Chemical** sensors in the **nose**. This is the sense of **smell**.

- **Pressure** and **temperature** sensors in the **skin**.

Human reproduction

Changes in females at puberty	Changes in males at puberty
• Breasts develop. • Pubic hair grows. • Hair grows under the arms. • Periods start – this is called menstruation. • The body grows. • The ovaries start to produce two hormones that control reproduction in females.	• The voice deepens. • Hair is produced around the body. • Hair around the sex organs is called pubic hair. • The testes produce sperm and the male sex hormone. • The body grows.

Summary of menstruation

DAY 1 – 5	The lining is lost from the uterus. This is called a period.
DAY 6 – 13	The lining of the uterus thickens ready for an embryo.
DAY 14	Ovulation occurs. A mature egg (ovum) is released from an ovary.
DAY 15	The ovum travels along the fallopian tube (oviduct) where it may be fertilised by a sperm. Usually fertilisation does not occur and the ovum dies.
DAY 16 – 21	The hormones in the female's body start to alter.
DAY 22 – 28	The lining of the uterus stops developing.
DAY 29 – 1	The lining of the uterus breaks down and is passed out of the vagina. This is a period. The cycle starts again.

If an ovum is fertilised on day 14 then the lining of the uterus develops into the placenta which will feed and protect the embryo. No more periods will occur nor will eggs be released until after the baby is born.

Drugs

These are any chemicals that have an effect on the body when taken in. They can be:

• Useful – e.g. paracetamol – pain relief, antibiotics – kill microbes.

• Harmful – e.g. nicotine – dependence on cigarettes, alcohol – liver problems.

• Very dangerous – e.g. paracetamol – can be fatal with overdose, heroin – addictive, cocaine – addictive – withdrawal problems – very hard to quit.

Drug misuse

The effect of drugs on a person depends upon the person's state of health and mind. The same drug can affect two different people in very different ways.

Solvents

- Seriously affect behaviour, the drug takes control.

- Damage to liver, lungs and brain.

- Most deaths are caused by inhaling vomit when unconscious.

Tobacco

- Nicotine is addictive – affects the blood pressure – calms people down – hard to give up.

- Other chemicals in cigarettes cause cancer of the throat, lungs and stomach.

- Causes breathing problems – emphysema, bronchitis.

- Carbon monoxide is in smoke – so the blood carries less oxygen – blood pressure is increased.

- Heart and blood vessels affected – heart disease, arterial disease.

Alcohol

- Affects the nervous system – in small amounts is a mild anaesthetic – slows reactions.

- Larger amounts – affects motor control – movement, speech – person is not in control.

- Coma (unconsciousness) may follow – can be fatal.

- Heavy drinking for a long time causes severe liver damage – cirrhosis – death can result – brain damage also.

Variation, inheritance and evolution

Variation

Living things look like their parents. They have similar characteristics. This is because their parents passed on information in their **genes** when sexual reproduction took place. Genes are carried on **chromosomes**.

Each parent passes on an equal amount of information to their offspring.

Genes control all characteristics of all living things.

Differences in living things are caused by:

- Different genes passed on from parents — these are **genetic** differences.

- The **environment** — these are the conditions in which a living thing develops.

Genetics and DNA

Genes are made from a chemical called DNA.

Male or Female?

In humans, whether you are male or female is controlled by two **chromosomes**.

- Males have the chromosomes **XY**.

- Females have the chromosomes **XX**.

Evolution

Evidence comes from **fossils** which are found in rocks. Fossils show us how living things have changed, or stayed the same, over millions of years.

Formation of fossils

- The hard parts of animals and plants do not decay easily.
- They are covered by sand/silt.
- The hard parts are replaced over millions of years by minerals in rocks.
- The animal/plant becomes a rock – a fossil.
- Sometimes fossils are formed from soft tissues which did not decay. This is because the microbes that decay matter were absent, or there was no oxygen to help the decay process.

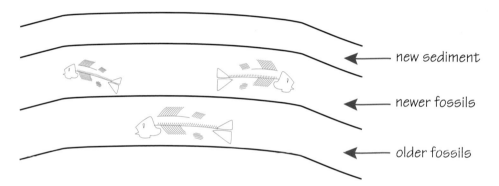

new sediment

newer fossils

older fossils

Life evolved over **3,000 million years ago** – living things today evolved from living things from the past – life evolved from the first simple living things.

Evolution takes millions of years and many animals and plants have become extinct. The changes in living things are shown in the fossil record – this is the evidence that supports the theory of evolution.

Extinction may be caused by:

- Environmental changes – the living thing can no longer survive – no food, water, etc.

- New predators – all the members of the species are eaten.

- Disease wiping out the population.

- New competitors – other animals are better at finding food, so no food is left for this species.

Humans as organisms and
Variation, inheritance and evolution

Questions

1 What are the main sources of carbohydrate? _____

2 What are the main sources of protein? _____

3 What are the main sources of fat? _____

4 What is fibre useful for? _____

5 Why does the body need iron? _____

6 Why does the body need calcium? _____

7 Do arteries carry blood towards or away from the heart? _____

8 Why do arteries have thick muscular walls? _____

9 Why do veins have valves? _____

10 What is the function of red blood cells? _____

11 Name three things carried by blood plasma. _____

12 Where in the lungs does oxygen enter the blood? _____

13 What is the food used in aerobic respiration? _____

14 What are the three functions of the skeleton? _____

_____

15 Which cells co-ordinate human behaviour? _____

16 Where do you find sensors for balance in your body? _____

17 Where do you find pressure and temperature sensors in the body?

_____

18 On which day of the menstrual cycle does ovulation occur?

_____

19 Name a drug that can be used as a common pain-killer.

_____

20 What do we call the drugs that are used to destroy microbes in the body?

_____

21 Which chromosomes determine sex in males? _____

22 Which chromosomes determine sex in females? _____

23 How long ago did life evolve on Earth? _____

24 How long does it take a fossil to form? _____

Green plants as organisms

Structure of plants

Plants have:

- **Roots** which anchor them to the ground.

- **Stems** to transport water and minerals to the leaves and flowers. The stem also transports food from the leaves to the roots.

- **Leaves** which use light, carbon dioxide and water to make food by **photosynthesis**.

- **Flowers** which are the reproductive organs.

Reproduction in plants

The flower

This consists of:

- **Receptacle** – where the flower develops.

- **Sepals** – protect the flower when it is a bud.

- **Petals** – brightly coloured to attract insects.

- **Stamens** – the male parts.

- **Carpels** – the female parts.

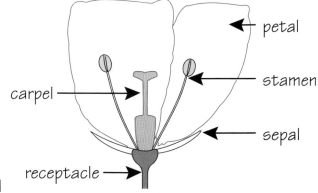

Female parts

Carpels are the female sex organs. Carpels have:

- **Stigma** – where the pollen lands.

- **Style** – connects the stigma to the ovary.

- **Ovary** – where the ovules are made and fertilised.

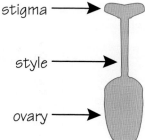

Male parts

These are the **stamens**.

Stamens consist of:

- **Anther** – where the pollen is made.

- **Filament** – the stalk that holds the anther in the air.

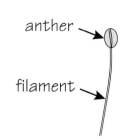

anther

filament

Pollination

This is where pollen is transferred from an **anther** to a **stigma**.

- **Cross-pollination** – pollen is transferred from one plant to another of the same species.

- **Self-pollination** – pollen is transferred from the anther on one plant to the stigma on the same plant.

Wind pollination

- Wind blows pollen from feathery anthers to sticky stigmas.

- Pollen is very light – some even has tiny wings to help it fly!

- The plant produces millions of pollen grains.

- This pollen is responsible for **hay fever**.

Insect pollination

- Pollen is large – it is a good food supply.

- Pollen can be sticky – to stick to insect/animal bodies.

- Not so much pollen is produced.

Fertilisation

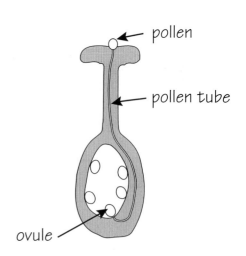

- Pollen lands on stigma.

- The pollen grows a **tube**.

- The tube grows through the style to the ovary.

- The pollen nucleus travels down the tube.

- The male sex cell in the pollen **fertilises** the female sex cell in the ovule.

Photosynthesis

You must learn this equation.

Plants make food by **photosynthesis**:

$$\text{carbon dioxide + water} \xrightarrow[\text{light}]{\text{chlorophyll}} \text{glucose + oxygen}$$

Photosynthesis is controlled by **enzymes**.
All enzyme reaction rates are variable depending on the conditions.

Carbon dioxide

- This is absorbed by the leaves by the process of diffusion through stomata.

- It is the plant's source of carbon to make food.

Light

- Light is absorbed by the leaves.

- Light is absorbed by the green chemical called **chlorophyll**.

- If there is little light there will be less photosynthesis.

Photosynthesis and assimilation

- **Assimilation** means **how food is used**.

- **Glucose** is used in **respiration** to **produce energy**, just as in animals.

In plants, the sugars produced by photosynthesis are used to:

- Produce **starch** which is stored as a future energy/raw material store.

- Convert into **cellulose** to make cell walls.

- Convert into **protein**, with the addition of nitrogen.

Transport and water relations – transpiration

- Plants absorb most of their water through root hair cells.

- A plant loses water through its leaves.

- The water that is lost from the leaves is replaced by water from the roots.

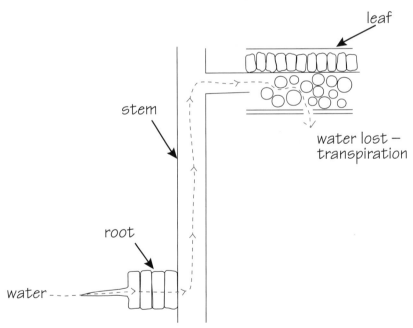

This movement of water is called the **transpiration stream** – it is fastest on hot, windy, dry, sunny days – it slows down on cold, wet, dark days.

Water is very important to all plants as it is needed for:

- Photosynthesis.

- Support – plant cells need water for support. Without water plants wilt. This is very important in young plants.

Green plants as organisms

Questions

1   Which part of a plant stops it being blown over? _____

2   Which part of a plant transports water to the leaves and food to the roots?

_____

3   Which part of the plant carries out photosynthesis? _____

4   Which part of the plant carries out reproduction? _____

5   Where is carbon dioxide absorbed by the plant? _____

6   Where is water absorbed by the plant? _____

7   Which part of a flower attracts insects? _____

8   What are the male sex organs of a plant called? _____

9   What are the female sex organs of a plant called? _____

10 What is responsible for hay fever? _____

11 Which part of the flower collects pollen after pollination? _____

12 Where does fertilisation in plants take place? _____

13 Which gas is used in photosynthesis? _____

14 Which gas is a waste product of photosynthesis? _____

15 What is the green colouring in plants called? _____

16 Which food is produced by plants as a result of photosynthesis?

_____

17 What is the name of the process whereby plants lose water?

_____

18 Where do plants lose water from? _____

19 Give two reasons why plants need water.

_____

20 Describe the weather when you would expect plants to lose most water.

_____

21 What is assimilation? _____

22 Why do plants need to respire? _____

23 Briefly describe how the sugars that a plant produces during photosynthesis are used.

_____

_____

Living things and their environment

Competition

Examiner's
tips and
your notes

You may be
asked to
interpret
unseen
information
– learn how
plants and
animals
compete!

**Living things live where the conditions suit them best.
They are often in competition with each other.**

Plants compete for:

- **Space** – to spread their leaves – to attract insects to flowers.

- **Light** – so their leaves can photosynthesise and make food.

- **Water and soil nutrients** – to keep their cells alive and for photosynthesis.

Animals compete for:

- **Water** – most animals need to drink. A few desert animals do not need to drink – e.g. the desert rat gets all the water it needs from its food. It is very well adapted to living in the desert and is one of the few animals to live in very dry areas.

- **Food** – all animals need food. Some eat plants and are called **herbivores**. Plants don't run away but animals compete with each other for the plants. Herbivores often live in large groups for protection. Some animals eat other animals. These are **carnivores**. Carnivores are also called **predators** and the animals they eat are their **prey**.

- **Space** – this is the area that an animal needs to find all its food and water and to breed successfully. The area where living things are found is called a **habitat**.

Populations

A population is the total number of one type of living thing in a whole community. The population of living things can be affected by:

- **Food** – more food = more living things, less food = fewer living things.

LIFE PROCESSES AND LIVING THINGS

- **Competition for food** – the more animal species that are competing for food resources, the fewer animals there will be in each species population. For example if voles and mice are competing for seeds there will be fewer mice or voles because less food is available for each species.
  Plants compete for soil nutrients in the same way.

- **Competition for light** – photosynthesis is affected by lack of light – e.g. ground plants in a forest are starved of light by tall trees. The ground may be quite bare. If a tree falls there may be an explosion of growth on the ground until a new tree grows to fill the gap.

- **Grazing** – plant populations are restricted by herbivores. In Africa different animals feed on different parts of the same plant.

- **Predation** – prey animal populations are controlled by predators. This population control is important as herbivores could eat all the food if there were too many of them. Then all of the animals would starve.

- **Disease** – a viral or bacterial disease could devastate a population. Disease does not usually kill every member of a species. Some individuals will be resistant and they will breed, which will lead to recovery of the population.

Energy and nutrient transfer

- Plants are called **producers** – they produce the food with light energy from the sun.

- Animals are called **consumers** – they consume the food.

Food chains

These link all the living things together.

E.g. A mouse eats some grass. The mouse is eaten by an owl. This is a food chain.

Arrows must point in the correct direction.

GRASS —EATEN BY→ MOUSE —EATEN BY→ OWL

- The arrow shows the direction that energy is moving.

- All food chains start with a green plant.

- All food chains end with an animal – usually a predator.

- The source of energy for all food chains is the Sun.

Food web

Food chains can be linked together. For example, grass is also eaten by insects and voles. Shrews eat insects. Owls eat shrews and voles.

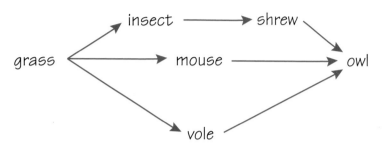

Food pyramids

This is a way of showing how many living things there are in a food chain, or how much mass there is in a food chain.

E.g. food chain – grass ⟶ mouse ⟶ owl

You need to be able to draw **food chains, pyramids of numbers** and **pyramids of biomass,** from information given.

pyramid of numbers

| owl |
| mouse |
| grass |

lots of grass

pyramid of biomass

| owl |
| mouse |
| grass |

tons of grass

E.g. food chain – tree ⟶ insect ⟶ robin

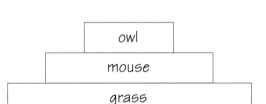

pyramid of numbers

| robin |
| insect |
| tree |

only 1 tree!

pyramid of biomass

| robin |
| insect |
| tree |

the tree is massive – very heavy

Classification of living things

Animals

These are divided into **invertebrates** and **vertebrates**.

Invertebrates
Do not have a backbone. The names of the groups are:

- **Protozoa** – single cells so all microscopic – e.g. amoeba.

- **Coelenterates** – have stinging cells and primitive soft bodies – e.g. jellyfish, sea anemone.

- **Flatworms** – e.g. tapeworm.

- **Annelid worm** – first group of animals to have segmented bodies – e.g. earthworm, leech.

- **Molluscs** – large group – have many different forms – all have soft bodies – most have a shell – e.g. snail, mussel, limpet (have shells), slug, octopus (no shell), cuttlefish, squid (small shell inside body).

- **Arthropods** – all have an external skeleton of hard material – exoskeleton. They have jointed limbs and most have antennae. There are four groups:

  1. **Crustaceans** – most live in sea, many legs, two pairs of antennae – e.g. crab, lobster, prawn and woodlouse (a land crustacean!).
  2. **Insects** – six legs, wings, three body parts, one pair of antennae, compound eyes – e.g. fly, bee, beetle.
  3. **Arachnids** – eight legs, two body parts, many simple eyes – e.g. spider, scorpion.
  4. **Myriapods** – many legs and body segments – e.g. millipede, centipede.

- **Echinoderms** – e.g. starfish, sea urchin.

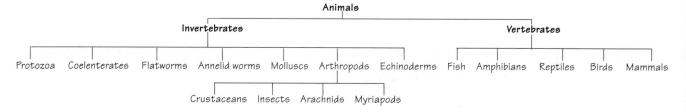

Vertebrates

Have a backbone. **Cold blooded vertebrates do not produce heat inside their bodies**. The groups are:

- **Fish** – streamlined, live in water, breathe using gills, lay soft eggs in water – e.g. cod, pike, shark, seahorse, whaleshark.

- **Amphibians** – live on land and in water, smooth slimy skin, breathe through skin, have lungs, use gills when tadpoles, lay soft eggs in water – e.g. newt, frog, toad, salamander.

- **Reptiles** – have dry scaly skin, breathe air using lungs, lay soft shelled eggs on land – e.g. snakes, lizards, alligators, crocodiles.

Warm blooded vertebrates produce heat inside their bodies. The groups are:

- **Birds** – have feathers, beaks and wings – most fly, lay hard shelled eggs on land – e.g. penguin, ostrich, finch, eagle.

- **Mammals** – have fur or hair, feed young on milk from mammary glands, most produce young that develop inside the female's body – e.g. human, cow, dog, whale, dolphin, duck-billed platypus (very primitive – lays eggs), kangaroo (marsupial mammal – young born immature and develop inside a pouch).

Plants

These have chlorophyll and there are two types – seed producers and those which do not produce seeds.

Seedless

- **Algae** – can be microscopic, primitive green plants, live in water, produce 80% of the Earth's oxygen as there are so many of them on the surface of the oceans – e.g. spirogyra, seaweed.

- **Mosses and liverworts** – no true roots, stems or leaves, small, live on land – e.g. bog moss.

- **Ferns** – have roots, stems and leaves, reproduce using spores – e.g. horsetail, bracken.

Seed producers

- **Gymnosperms** – conifers – reproduce using cones, no true flowers but cones have seeds – e.g. larch, pine.

- **Angiosperms** – flowering plants, have flowers and produce seeds (see section on plants, page 26) – e.g. rose, oak, buttercup.

Viruses

- Only survive inside living cells. Scientists still argue if they are truly alive. Very small – e.g. cold, HIV, flu are caused by viruses.

Bacteria

- Microscopic, most can live on their own. Most are very useful, only a minority cause disease – e.g. streptococci (sore throats), tetanus, T.B.

Fungi

- Most are microscopic – they are NOT plants – no chlorophyll. Most are decomposers in the soil, very useful – e.g. mushroom, toadstool, yeast. A few cause disease – e.g. some species of yeast.

Living things and their environment

Questions

1   Name three factors which can affect the population of living things.

_____

2   Why do plants need light? _____

3   Why do plants need water? _____

4   What is a herbivore? _____

5   What is a carnivore? _____

6   What is a predator? _____

7   What is meant by the term 'a population of animals'? _____

_____

8   What effect would increasing the food supply have on the
population of a group of animals? _____

9   What effect would increasing competition for food have on the
population of a group of animals? _____

10   What effect would an increased number of predators have on the
population of a group of prey animals? _____

11   What do all food chains start with? _____

12   In a food chain, what is a producer? _____

13   In a food chain, what is a consumer? _____

14   What is the ultimate source of energy in all food chains? _____

15   A woodlouse eats dead leaves and centipedes eat woodlice.
Write the food chain below.

_____

16   Sketch and label a pyramid of numbers and a pyramid of
biomass for the above food chain.

17   What are animals with backbones called? _____

18   Which group of animals have wings and six legs? _____

19   What type of animal is a snake? _____

Life processes and living things • Answers

Life processes and cell activity

1 sensitivity   2 respiration   3 excretion   4 reproduction
5 growth   6 animals   7 moving reproduction sensitivity
feeding excretion respiration growth   8 cytoplasm
9 nucleus   10 cellulose cell wall   11 chloroplast   12 vacuole
13 tissue   14 organ   15 system   16 organism
17 chloroplast/cellulose cell wall   18 cell   19 organ   20 organ

Humans as organisms and Variation, inheritance and evolution

1 vegetables/bread/cakes/sweets   2 meat/fish/eggs/milk
products   3 butter/margarine/full milk   4 digestion/prevents
constipation   5 make red blood cells   6 make bones   7 away
8 withstand high pressure   9 keep blood flowing one way/stop
backflow of blood   10 carry oxygen   11 carbon dioxide/
heat/glucose/antibodies/hormones (any 3)   12 alveoli
13 glucose   14 support/protection/make blood cells   15 nerves
16 ears   17 skin   18 fourteen   19 paracetamol/aspirin
20 antibiotics   21 XY   22 XX   23 3,000 million years
24 millions of years

Green plants as organisms

1 roots   2 stem   3 leaves   4 flowers   5 leaves   6 roots
7 petals   8 stamens   9 carpels   10 pollen   11 stigma
12 ovary   13 carbon dioxide   14 oxygen   15 chlorophyll
16 glucose/starch   17 transpiration   18 leaves
19 photosynthesis and support/strength   20 windy and warm
21 how food is used   22 produce energy   23 energy to
grow/produce seeds/store food

Living things and their environment

1 space/water/competition for food or light/environmental changes/disease (any 3)   2 photosynthesis   3 strength or support and photosynthesis   4 animal eats plants   5 animal eats animals   6 animals that hunt   7 number of living things of that species   8 increase it   9 decrease it   10 decrease it
11 plants   12 plant   13 animal   14 Sun
15 leaves ————> woodlouse ————> centipede
16

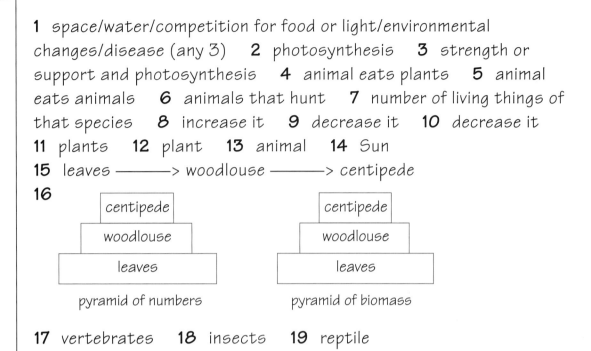

pyramid of numbers   pyramid of biomass

17 vertebrates   18 insects   19 reptile

Materials and their properties

Materials and their uses

Apparatus

The shape and function of various pieces of laboratory apparatus:

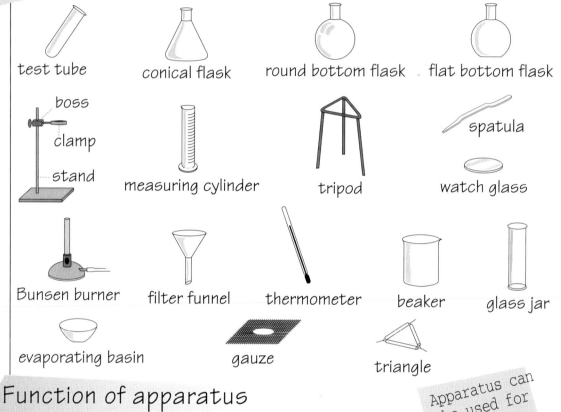

Function of apparatus

- Test tube – heating solids and liquids.

- Conical flask – heating liquids, collecting filtrates.

- Round and flat bottom flasks – heating liquids.

- Filter funnel – separating solids from liquids.

- Beaker – heating and boiling liquids.

- Stand, boss and clamp – supporting apparatus in place.

- Measuring cylinder – measuring the volume of liquids.

- Watch glass – collecting and evaporating liquids with no heat.

- Evaporating dish – collecting and evaporating liquids with heat.

- Spatula – handling solid chemicals.

- Tripod – supporting apparatus above a Bunsen burner.

- Gauze – spreading heat from Bunsen burner and supporting apparatus on a tripod.

Apparatus can be used for various functions. 'Function to fit the job' should be your guideline.

- Gas jar – collecting gases for testing.

- Thermometer – measuring temperature of substances.

- Bunsen burner – heating apparatus in a laboratory.

Hazard labels on chemical jars

oxidising agent   flammable   explosive   corrosive

harmful/irritant   toxic   radioactive

- **Oxidising agent** – helps other things to burn.

- **Highly inflammable** – this will catch fire if it is near a flame.

- **Explosive** – this substance can explode.

- **Toxic** – this is poisonous. It could kill us if we swallow it or even touch it. Some of these substances can pass through your skin and poison you!

- **Harmful** – be careful, this may cause harm.

- **Irritant** – this will cause your skin or eyes to become sore or itchy.

- **Corrosive** – this can cause serious skin burns. It will damage furniture. You **must** wear protective glasses.

- **Radioactive** – gives off ionising radiation that can be harmful.

Examples of harmful chemicals

- Irritant – bromine, ammonia, dilute acid, dilute alkali.

- Radioactive – plutonium, uranium.

- Oxidising agent – potassium nitrate, sodium chlorate.

- Toxic – sodium cyanide, copper sulphate, mercury.

- Explosive – potassium, petrol vapour.

- Flammable – acetone, ethanol, petrol.

- Corrosive – concentrated acids, concentrated alkalis, bromine.

Some chemicals can have more than one hazard label.

Solids, liquids and gases

All substances exist in three physical states – solids, liquids and gases.

The most common of substances, water, exists in these forms:

ice	–	solid
water	–	liquid
steam	–	gas

Changes in states of matter

Remember the only difference in these three forms of substance is the amount of energy which particles have, in this case heat.

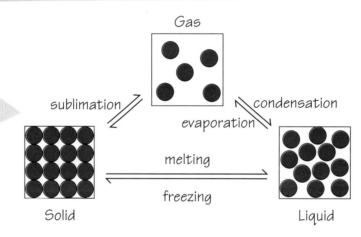

This is a physical process, not a chemical reaction.

Properties of solids, liquids and gases:

- **Solids** – have a definite volume and shape, cannot be compressed.

- **Liquids** – have a definite volume but take up the shape of their container, cannot be compressed.

- **Gases** – have no definite volume or shape, take up as much room as the container allows and take up the shape of the container. Will expand or contract as the container does, can be compressed.

Substances are made of particles. These particles move. The higher the energy level, the quicker the particles move:

- **Solids** – particles are close together and vibrate slowly relative to one another.

- **Liquids** – particles are more loosely linked. They can slide against each other so that liquids can flow. The particles move more quickly than they do in solids.

- **Gases** – particles are not linked or are very loosely linked, they move very quickly.

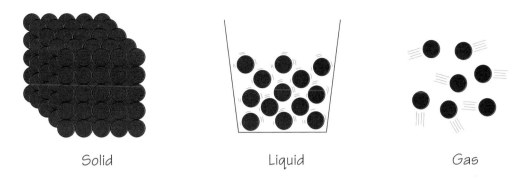

Solid   Liquid   Gas

Separation

Substances can be separated in several ways. To achieve this, differences between them must be found.

Filtration

A solid can be separated from a liquid by filtering through a filter paper using a filter funnel.

- Examples of using filtration – separating sand from water, soil from water and glass from water. **Difference is solid/liquid**.

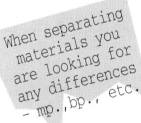

When separating materials you are looking for any differences – mp., bp., etc.

Distillation

Liquids can be separated from dissolved solids by simple distillation.

Simple distillation

thermometer
water out
condenser
liquid evaporating
water in
heat
distillate

Fractional distillation

thermometer
fractioning column
water out
condenser
water in
distillate
liquid evaporating
heat

Liquids can be separated from liquids by fractional distillation.

- Examples of simple distillation (solids from liquids) – water from ink and water from any salt solution e.g. sea water. **Difference is solid/liquid.**

- Examples of fractional distillation (liquids from liquids) – alcohol from water, petrol from oil. **Difference is boiling point.**

Centrifuge

- Separation of solids from liquids, faster than filtering. Scientists use a centrifuge to separate the different parts of blood to test for disease and illness.

Chromatography

- Coloured substances can be separated using chromatography. Used by scientists in forensic investigations and in DNA analysis. Substances can be coloured artificially.

Solutions

- A solution can be a mixture of a liquid and a solid – e.g. sea water is a mixture of salt (solid) and water (liquid). It can also be a mixture of liquids – e.g. beer is a mixture of water and alcohol with flavouring.

- **Solution** – a mixture of a solid and a liquid where the solid has dissolved in the liquid.

- **Solute** – the solid which dissolves in a solvent to form a solution.

- **Solvent** – a liquid in which the solute dissolves to become a solution.

An everyday example of a solution is a cup of tea.

solute (sugar)   dissolve

solvent (tea)   solution

Mixtures and compounds

- A mixture contains two or more substances that can be separated quite easily — e.g. a mixture of sand and iron can be separated using a magnet.

- When two or more elements are chemically combined (joined together) to produce a compound, they can only be separated with difficulty — e.g. water is a compound containing two elements, hydrogen and oxygen.

Name of substance	Type	Separation	Particles present
water	compound	difficult	hydrogen and oxygen
ammonia	compound	difficult	nitrogen and hydrogen
carbon dioxide	compound	difficult	carbon and oxygen
iron/sulphur	mixture	easy, using magnet	iron and sulphur
sand/sugar	mixture	easy, dissolve sugar in water and filter	many different ones
sea water	mixture	easy, distil to get pure water	many different ones

Materials and their uses

Questions

1 What are the following pieces of apparatus used for:
   (a) Round bottomed flask? _____
   (b) Measuring cylinder? _____
   (c) Spatula? _____
   (d) Gauze? _____
   (e) Watch glass? _____

2 What do the following hazard warning labels tell you about the chemical in the jar? Give one example of a chemical that would be in a jar with each label.

    (a)   (b)   (c)   (d)

(a) _____
(b) _____
(c) _____
(d) _____

3 List the three states of matter.
   (a) _____
   (b) _____
   (c) _____

4 What changes the states of matter from one to another?

_____

5 Name three ways in which matter can be changed from one state to another.
   (a) _____
   (b) _____
   (c) _____

6 Write down three properties of a gas.
   (a) _____
   (b) _____
   (c) _____

7 Name the process (method) you would use to separate:
   (a) a solid from a liquid. _____
   (b) a dissolved solid from a solution. _____

8 What process would you use to separate a mixture of coloured dyes? _____

9 In which state could a substance flow and have a definite surface? _____

10 What process could be used to separate alcohol from a mixture of alcohol and water? _____
Why does this work? _____

11 Fill in the spaces in the following passage using the words listed below. Each word may be used more than once or even not at all.

SOLUTION   SOLUTE   DISSOLVED   SOLVENT   DISSOLVES
EVAPORATION   EVAPORATING   SUBLIMATION
CONDENSATION   CONDENSING

When salt is _____ in water it becomes a salt _____. The water is called a _____ because it _____ the salt. The salt can be recovered from the _____ by _____ the water leaving the salt behind. An _____ dish can be used for this process. The water can be obtained from the salt _____ by _____ and then _____ in a condenser. When sugar is _____ in tea it is a _____ and the tea is a _____.

Properties of materials

Types of material

- Materials can be divided into two types – **natural** and **artificial**.

- Natural materials are those that are found in nature. They do not need changing by people to be used.

- Artificial materials have been manufactured, usually chemically, in order to be used.

Artificial, synthetic and man-made all mean the same thing when talking about materials.

Examples of natural and artificial materials:

Natural	Artificial	Natural	Artificial
crude oil	petrol	stone	cement
wood	paper	air	plastics
wool	wax	water	beer

- List five natural and artificial materials that you use.

Elements

- **Materials that contain just one type of atom are called elements** – e.g. carbon contains only carbon atoms.

- There are about 106 elements.

- There are 92 natural elements. The rest are artificial.

All elements have symbols – here are just a few:

Oxygen	O	Hydrogen	H	Nitrogen	N
Carbon	C	Copper	Cu	Sodium	Na
Iron	Fe	Neon	Ne	Chlorine	Cl
Magnesium	Mg	Fluorine	F	Potassium	K

Chemical and physical processes

- When ice turns to water or water turns to steam this is a **physical** process.

- When magnesium burns it takes up oxygen. This is a **chemical** reaction.

- Wax melting is a **physical** process.

- Wax burning is a **chemical** reaction.

PHYSICAL CHANGE	CHEMICAL CHANGE
Easy to turn back.	Difficult to change back.
New substance **not** formed.	New substance formed.
No change in weight.	Substances change in weight.

The Periodic Table

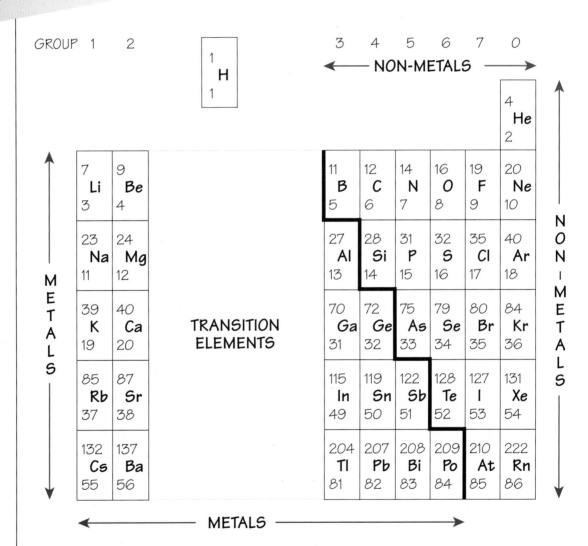

GROUP 1   2   3   4   5   6   7   0

NON-METALS

METALS

NON-METALS

TRANSITION ELEMENTS

METALS

Patterns in the Periodic Table

Group 1 elements are called the alkaline metals. Group 7 elements are called the halogens. Group 8 elements are called the noble gases.

- The Periodic Table is separated into metals and non-metals.

- In the boxes with the symbol for each element are two numbers — e.g. carbon is $^{12}_{6}C$. The number at the bottom left of the symbol ($_{6}C$) is the **atomic number**. The number at the top left of the symbol (^{12}C) is the **atomic mass**.

- Along the top are numbers 1 to 0 over the vertical columns — these columns are called groups or families — e.g. Group 1 is Li, Na, K, Rb, Cs and Fr.

- A row across is a **period** — e.g. Li, Be, B, C, N, O, F and Ne.

- Elements are arranged in order of atomic number in the Periodic Table.

- Elements with similar properties line up in the vertical columns or groups.

- There are 8 groups in the Periodic Table.

- Metals are good conductors of heat and electricity. They are shiny, malleable (can be hammered into shapes) and ductile (can be drawn out into wires). Most are hard, dense and have high melting points.

- Iron, cobalt and nickel are magnetic metals.

- Most non-metals are gases.

- Non-metals usually have low melting and boiling points. They are usually poor conductors of heat and electricity. (*Note* — graphite — a form of carbon — conducts both heat and electricity.) If solid, they are usually dull and brittle — e.g. sulphur.

Acids and alkalis

When a substance dissolves in water to form a solution it will become **acidic**, **alkaline** or **neutral**.

the pH Scale

	strong acid	weak acid			weak alkali		strong alkali
Colour	red	orange	yellow	green	blue	indigo	violet
pH Number	1	3 to 4	5 to 6	7	8 to 9	10 to 12	13 to 14

acidic ← → neutral ← → alkaline

The colour refers to the colour change in Universal Indicator.

Water is neutral

	phenolphthalein	litmus
Acid	colourless	red
Alkali	red	blue

Indigestion can be helped by neutralisation with a weak alkali, like chalk.

The table above indicates the colours shown by acids and alkalis in other indicators.

- When an acid is added to an alkali until pH 7 is reached, the acid and the alkali are said to have **neutralised** each other.

- This chemical reaction always gives the same products:

    acid   +   alkali ————> salt   +   water

- This process is called **neutralisation**.

- A salt in this case is not necessarily sodium chloride (common salt) although sodium chloride can be produced by this process.

- Common acids are – nitric acid, hydrochloric acid and sulphuric acid.

- Common alkalis are – sodium hydroxide, potassium hydroxide and ammonium hydroxide.

- Common salts are – sodium nitrate, potassium chloride and ammonium sulphate.

- Many acids react with reactive metals to produce salts and hydrogen:

    metal   +   acid ————> metal salt   +   hydrogen

- Acids react with carbonates to form salts and carbon dioxide:

    metal carbonate + acid ————> metal salt + carbon dioxide + water

- Acids react with metal oxides to produce salts and water:

    metal oxide   +   acid ————> metal salt   +   water

Air

The noble gases are: helium, argon, neon, krypton, xenon, radon.

Air is a mixture of gases. The pie chart indicates the gases present in the air and the quantity of each.

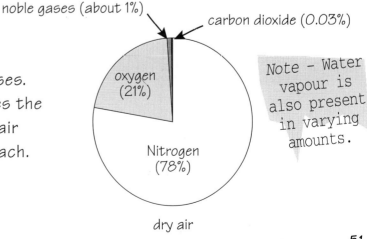

noble gases (about 1%)

carbon dioxide (0.03%)

oxygen (21%)

Nitrogen (78%)

dry air

Note – Water vapour is also present in varying amounts.

Many useful products are made from air:

Oxygen

- Used in welding – produces a hot flame.

- Used in hospitals – incubators for babies.

The noble gases are sometimes called the inert gases as they do not combine with anything.

Nitrogen

- Used when an inert (will not allow things to burn) atmosphere is required.

- In its liquid form it is used to keep chilled foods cool in lorries.

Carbon dioxide

- Does not support combustion and is used in some fire extinguishers.

- In its solid form it is also used as a coolant (see nitrogen).

Noble gases

- Helium is used in fairground balloons.

- Also used in airships which carry people.

- The main use for the other noble gases is in advertising lamps, where they give different colours.

Rusting

- When iron and steel come into contact with air and water they rust.

- The iron combines with the oxygen in the air to form iron oxide – we know this as rust.

- Both water and oxygen are needed to produce iron oxide.

Salt (sodium chloride) when added to water will increase the rate of rusting. That is why ships go rusty quickly when at sea.

The fire triangle

For something to burn three things are required:

heat / fuel

oxygen
(in the air)

Take one of these things away and the fire will go out.

Oxidation and reduction

This reaction occurs when iron is extracted from its ore in a **blast furnace**.

- When a substance burns it takes up oxygen – when iron takes up oxygen it goes rusty – these are examples of **oxidation**.

- If a substance loses oxygen it has been **reduced**.

One example of oxidation and reduction is when iron is produced from iron ore (iron(III)oxide):

$$\underbrace{iron(III)oxide \;+\; carbon\ monoxide \longrightarrow iron \;+\; carbon\ dioxide}_{}$$

reduction

$$Fe_2O_3 \quad + \quad 3CO \quad \longrightarrow \quad 2Fe \;+\; 3CO_2$$

oxidation

- In this reaction the iron oxide has been **reduced** to iron by losing oxygen to carbon monoxide.

- The carbon monoxide has been **oxidised** to carbon dioxide by taking the oxygen from the iron.

- Both oxidation and reduction processes take place in the same reaction.

Fuels

- A fuel is a substance that we burn to obtain its energy.

- Coal, oil and gas are fossil fuels.

- These fuels are made from vegetable and animal matter that lived and died millions of years ago – heat and pressure have turned them into fuels.

- Coal is carbon – oil and gas are hydrocarbons.

- They all burn to produce carbon dioxide – hydrocarbons produce water as well.

$$methane \;+\; oxygen \longrightarrow carbon\ dioxide \;+\; water$$
$$CH_4(g) \;+\; 2O_2(g) \longrightarrow CO_2(g) \;+\; 2H_2O(l)$$

- Burning coal produces ash and tarry substances that need to be disposed of.

- Oil, gas and coal contain sulphur which burns in air, forming sulphur dioxide. This is an acidic gas.

- Acid gases form acid rain when dissolved in rain water.

Properties of materials

Questions

1 Which of the following are natural materials? Underline your answers.
Crude oil, plastic, wool, stone, cement, petrol.

2 What is the name given to a substance which is made up of one type of atom only?

_____

3 Write down the chemical symbol for:
Carbon _____
Magnesium _____
Sodium _____
Potassium. _____

4 In which one of the following does a chemical change take place? Underline your answer.
Cutting grass, melting wax, boiling water, burning wood.

5 Look at the list of elements and choose the one which best fits each description below.
Carbon, nitrogen, aluminium, sulphur.
(a) it is shiny and can be polished.
(b) it is yellow and brittle.
(c) it is black and often hard.
(d) it is a gas at room temperature.

6 Vinegar – pH5, hydrochloric acid – pH1, sodium carbonate – pH8, sodium hydroxide – pH12.
Which of the above is:
(a) a weak acid? _____
(b) a strong alkali? _____

7 Which gas is produced when an acid reacts with a metal carbonate? _____

8 Which gas is produced when acid reacts with iron?_____

9 Name the indicator which is blue in alkali and red in acid. _____

10 What is the name given to the type of reaction which happens when an acid and an alkali react together to give a salt and water only? _____

11 How much of the air is oxygen? _____

12 Which noble gas is used in balloons? _____

13 In each of the following write down whether the process described is **oxidation** or **reduction**:
(a) burning a match in oxygen. _____
(b) removing oxygen from iron oxide to give iron. _____
(c) an apple which turns brown. _____

14 What is a fuel? A fuel is a _____.

15 Which two elements does the hydrocarbon methane contain?

_____

Chemical reactions

Examiner's tips and your notes

A chemical reaction can be represented using the word equation:

reactants ———> products

- The reactants are what you start with before the reaction.

- The products are the substances left after the reaction. For example, when magnesium burns in air:

magnesium + oxygen ———> magnesium oxide

- Magnesium and oxygen are the reactants.

- Magnesium oxide is the product.

State symbols are:
 s = solid,
 l = liquid,
 g = gas,
aq = dissolved in water.

Another example is when copper carbonate is heated:

copper carbonate(s) ———> copper oxide(s) + carbon dioxide(g)

Precipitation

- Most of the compounds that you use dissolve (i.e. are soluble) in water.

- If two chemicals that are soluble react to give an insoluble substance, this will come out of solution and sink to the bottom of the test tube — it is called a precipitate.

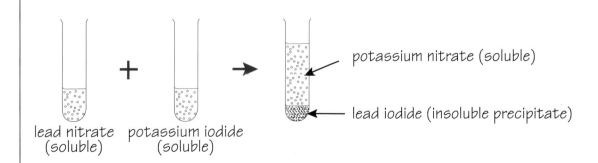

lead nitrate (soluble)   potassium iodide (soluble)

potassium nitrate (soluble)

lead iodide (insoluble precipitate)

This reaction can be represented in words by this equation:

lead nitrate(aq)+potassium iodide(aq) ———>potassium nitrate(aq)+lead iodide(s)↓

The arrow indicates that this product is a precipitate.

Reversible reactions

This is a chemical reaction, **not** a physical reaction, even though it can be reversed.

• Some reactions can be reversed:

Anydrous means 'without water'.

$$\text{copper sulphate} \rightleftharpoons \text{anhydrous copper sulphate} + \text{water}$$
$$\text{CuSO}_4.5\text{H}_2\text{O} \qquad\qquad \text{CuSO}_4 \qquad + \quad 5\text{H}_2\text{O}$$
$$\text{blue} \qquad\qquad\qquad\qquad \text{white}$$

The **two** arrows indicate the reaction is reversible.

This reaction can be used to detect small amounts of water. If the white copper sulphate goes blue, then water is present.

Displacement reactions

• In some reactions a metal will be pushed out of the solution by a more reactive metal.

• An example of this is when iron is added to a copper sulphate solution:

The iron is more reactive than the copper so takes its place.

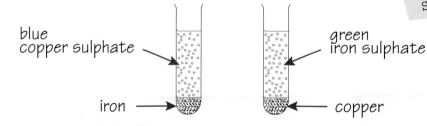

blue copper sulphate

green iron sulphate

iron

copper

copper sulphate + iron ———> copper + iron sulphate

• The copper has been displaced (pushed out) by the iron.

• The solid turns red/brown and the blue solution turns a light green.

• Iron is the more reactive metal, it is more reactive than copper.

Decomposition

- When some substances are heated they break down into other substances.

- An example of this is when copper carbonate is heated:

copper carbonate(s) ————> copper oxide(s) + carbon dioxide(g)
(green)   (black)   (colourless)

Synthesis

- The opposite of decomposition.

- It is the formation of new substances from elements or from simpler substances — e.g.

iron + sulphur ————> iron sulphide

- The compound iron sulphide has been synthesised from the elements iron and sulphur.

Mass in reactions

- The mass remains the same throughout a chemical reaction.

- Total mass of reactants = total mass of products.

- Matter can neither be destroyed nor created during a chemical reaction.

Sometimes it appears as though reactants disappear when a gas is produced during the reaction.

Endothermic and exothermic reactions

- Chemical reactions involve a change in energy.

- Chemical reactions can give out heat or need heat to take place.

- Exothermic reactions give out heat (causing an increase in temperature).

- Endothermic reactions take in heat (causing a decrease in temperature).

- Some exothermic reactions require energy to start them off – e.g. burning gas requires energy in the form of a spark to start it.

Endothermic starts with the same two letters as entrance, which means **in** (en = in).

- ΔH is negative for an exothermic reaction – e.g. $2Mg + O_2 \longrightarrow 2MgO - \Delta H$ (gives out heat)

- ΔH is positive for an endothermic reaction – e.g. $2NH_3 \longrightarrow N_2 + 3H_2 + \Delta H$ (heat taken in)

All combustion (burning in air) is exothermic.

- Energy is required in a reaction to break the bonds between atoms (endothermic).

- This energy is called bond energy.

Exothermic starts with the same two letters as exit – which means way **out** (exo = out).

- Energy is given out in a reaction to make new bonds between atoms (exothermic).

Reversible reactions

The **two** arrows indicate the reaction is reversible.

- Some reactions can be reversed.

- The products of these reactions can react to make the original reactants.

$$A + B \rightleftharpoons C + D$$

- These reactions never proceed fully from reactants to products.

This is a chemical reaction **not** a physical reaction, even though it can be reversed.

- **The reactants and products reach an equilibrium somewhere in between.**

- The reaction reaches a balance where reactants and products are being produced at an equal rate.

- This equilibrium depends upon the conditions of the reaction.

- If you change the conditions of the reaction the position of the equilibrium changes to **oppose** that change – e.g. if you increase the temperature the equilibrium changes to reduce the temperature.

- In an endothermic reaction, an increase in temperature will increase the yield of the products of reaction.

- In an exothermic reaction an increase in temperature will decrease the yield of the products of reaction.

- An example of a reversible reaction is:

$$\text{copper sulphate} \rightleftharpoons \text{copper sulphate} + \text{water}$$
$$CuSO_4.5H_2O \qquad\qquad CuSO_4 \qquad + 5H_2O$$
$$\text{blue} \qquad\qquad\qquad \text{white}$$

Electrolysis

Anode is the positive (+) electrode ('add' starts with 'a'), cathode is the negative (–) electrode.

- Electrolysis is the splitting up of compounds into other substances using electricity.

- Water can be broken down into its constituent elements of hydrogen and oxygen by passing an electrical current through the acidified water.

- Hydrogen comes off at the cathode and oxygen comes off at the anode.

- There is twice the volume of hydrogen as oxygen (therefore H_2O).

*If you put a **lighted** splint into a test tube full of hydrogen, it will explode with a squeaky pop – this is the test for hydrogen.*

*If you put a **glowing** splint into a test tube full of oxygen, it will relight – this is the test for oxygen.*

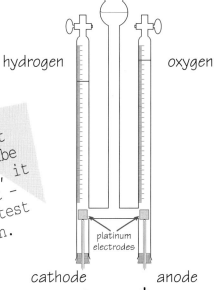

hydrogen   oxygen

platinum electrodes

cathode   anode
–   +

Electrolysis is used for the commercial plating of many objects.

- Sodium chloride (common salt) solution can be broken down into other substances by electricity:

You can detect the smell of bleach or swimming baths from the gas coming off at the cathode – this is chlorine.

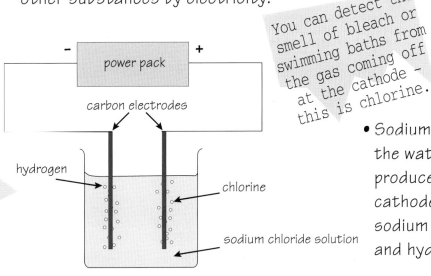

power pack

carbon electrodes

hydrogen

chlorine

sodium chloride solution

- Sodium reacts with the water when it is produced at the cathode, giving sodium hydroxide and hydrogen.

- This is the industrial process used to extract **sodium, chlorine and hydrogen from sodium chloride**, which is mined in Cheshire.

Chemical reactions

Questions

1 In a chemical reaction what are:
   (a) reactants? _____
   (b) products? _____

2 In the reaction:
   copper carbonate ———> copper oxide + carbon dioxide
   name a product. _____

3 A **precipitate** is formed when two soluble substances react
   together to give an _____

4 What is the name given to a chemical reaction which works in
   both directions such as:

   nitrogen   +   hydrogen $\rightleftharpoons$ ammonia

5 When an iron nail is placed in copper sulphate solution the iron
   becomes coated with copper.
   (a) Which is the more reactive metal – iron or copper?

   _____

   (b) What is the name given to this type of reaction?

   _____

6 Give an example of a thermal decomposition reaction.

   _____

7 What is the name given to a type of reaction in which elements
   join together to give a new substance? _____

8 Which one of the following is not true?
   (a) mass remains the same throughout a chemical reaction.
   (b) total mass of reactants = total mass of products.
   (c) matter can easily be destroyed in a chemical reaction.

   Number _____ is not true.

9 Complete the sentences
   (a) An exothermic reaction is one in which _____
       to the surroundings.
   (b) An endothermic reaction is one in which _____
       from the surroundings.

10 What type of reaction is always exothermic?

    _____

11 In electrolysis what name is given to:
    (a) the negative electrode? _____
    (b) the positive electrode? _____

12 When water is electrolysed which element is given off at:
    (a) the negative electrode? _____
    (b) the positive electrode? _____

13 Describe a test for hydrogen.

    _____

    _____

14 Describe the test for oxygen gas. _____

    _____

The structure of the Earth

The Earth is not made of the same material all the way through. It has:

- A thin crust that we live on.

- A mantle – this is molten rock.

- An outer core – this is made of molten nickel and iron.

Nickel and iron are magnetic metals. They give the Earth its magnetic field.

- The inner core – this is made of solid nickel and iron.

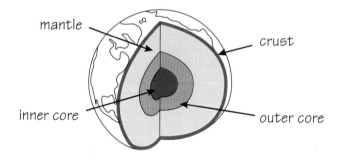

Volcanoes

Volcanoes have the general structure:

Molten rock underground is called magma. When it comes to the surface it is called lava.

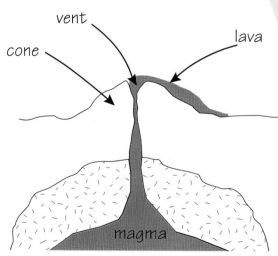

Plate tectonics

- The crust of the Earth is made up of plates 'floating' on the mantle.

- These plates are constantly moving and are moving in different directions.

- Where these plates slide against each other earthquakes occur – the San Andreas Fault is one example.

- Where these plates collide head on, one of the plates rides over the other and sends it back towards the centre of the Earth. This is the site of volcanic action and mountain ranges – the Andes in South America is one example of this.

- There is a fault down the centre of the Atlantic Ocean, moving the plates apart.

Types of rock

Igneous rocks:

$$\text{molten magma} \xrightarrow[\text{cooling}]{\text{fast}} \text{small crystals – e.g. basalt}$$

$$\text{molten magma} \xrightarrow[\text{cooling}]{\text{slow}} \text{large crystals – e.g. granite}$$

Sedimentary rocks:

$$\text{igneous rocks} \xrightarrow[\text{eroded}]{\text{weathered}} \text{layered and compressed – e.g. mudstone}$$

Metamorphic rocks:

$$\text{sedimentary rocks} \xrightarrow[\text{pressure}]{\text{heat}} \text{metamorphic rocks – e.g. marble}$$

The rock cycle

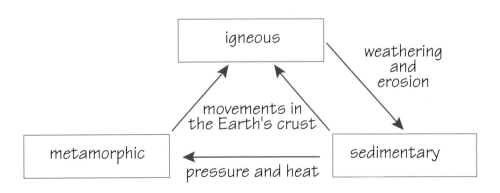

- Eroded rocks become soil when organic matter is mixed with them.

Rocks as raw materials

- All metals are obtained from rocks.

- Rocks can be used as building materials.

Weathering and erosion

There is a difference between weathering and erosion!

Agents of weathering are:

- The Sun
- Rain

Agents of erosion are:

- Rivers
- Freezing water

- Glaciers
- People

- The sea
- Wind

- Glaciers form 'U' shaped valleys
- Rivers form 'V' shaped valleys

Chemical weathering and erosion

- The burning of fossil fuels has increased the levels of acid gases in the atmosphere (sulphur dioxide, carbon dioxide and nitrogen oxides).

- Carbon dioxide forms a weak acid with rain which slowly dissolves rocks made of carbonates.

- Sulphur is present in oil and coal.

- When sulphur is burned it forms sulphur dioxide.

- This oxide of sulphur dissolves in rain to give a strong acid.

- Acid rain dissolves rocks as they are found in nature and the ones we use for buildings.

The structure of the Earth

Questions

1 Name three agents of erosion.

_____

_____

_____

2 Label the diagram of the Earth below.

3 What two substances are contained in the Earth's core?

_____

_____

4 What name is given to the molten rock which:
(a) is inside a volcano? _____
(b) flows out of a volcano? _____

5 What happens when two tectonic plates slide against each other?
It produces an _____

6 Name an igneous rock. _____

7 Name a sedimentary rock. _____

8 Name a metamorphic rock. _____

9 How is a sedimentary rock such as coal formed?

_____

_____

_____

10 What elements are always obtained from rocks?

_____

Materials and their properties • Answers

Materials and their uses

1 a) heating liquids b) measuring the volume of a liquid
c) spatula means – spoon – it is used to 'spoon' solids d) gauze –
to spread heat onto and support glassware e) watch glass – to
evaporate small amounts of liquid at room temperature
2 a) oxidising agent – oxygen b) flammable – petrol c) explosive –
liquid petroleum gas d) corrosive – hydrochloric acid   **3** a) solid
b) liquid c) gas   **4** addition or removal of heat (raising or lowering
temperature)   **5** a) solid ——> liquid – melting b) liquid ——>
gas – boiling or evaporation c) gas ——> liquid – condensation
6 a) compressible   b) fills the whole container   c) particles widely
spread   **7** a) filtration b) evaporation   **8** chromatography
9 liquid   **10** Distillation works because the boiling points of the
two liquids are different   **11** When salt is **dissolved** in water it
becomes a salt **solution**. The water is called a **solvent** because it
dissolves the salt. The salt can be recovered from the **solution** by
evaporating the water leaving the salt behind. An **evaporating** dish
can be used for this process. The water can be obtained from the
salt **solution** by **evaporation** and then **condensation** in a condenser.
When sugar is **dissolved** in tea it is a **solute** and the tea is a
solvent.

Properties of materials

1 crude oil, wool, stone   **2** an element   **3** carbon = C;
magnesium = Mg; sodium = Na and potassium = K   **4** burning
wood. All the others are physical charges.   **5** a) aluminium
b) sulphur c) carbon d) nitrogen   **6** a) vinegar   b) sodium
hydroxide   **7** carbon dioxide gas   **8** hydrogen gas   **9** litmus
10 neutralisation   **11** 21%   **12** helium   **13** a) oxidation
b) reduction   c) oxidation   **14** A fuel is a substance which burns
to release heat and light energy.   **15** hydrogen and carbon

Chemical reactions

1 a) substances which react together   b) substances produced by the reaction   2 either copper oxide or carbon dioxide
3 insoluble substance   4 reversible   5 a) iron b) displacement
6 copper carbonate $\xrightarrow{\text{heat}}$ copper oxide + carbon dioxide
7 synthesis   8 letter c) is not true   9 a) gives out heat
b) takes heat in   10 combustion or burning in air   11 a) cathode
b) anode   12 a) hydrogen b) oxygen   13 it burns with a
'squeaky' pop when lit   14 oxygen relights a glowing wooden splint

The structure of the Earth

1 rivers, freezing water, glaciers, people, wind or sea
2 A = mantle, B = crust, C = inner core, D = outer core   3 nickel
or iron   4 a) magma b) lava   5 earthquake   6 basalt or
granite   7 limestone, chalk or mudstone   8 marble
9 particles of eroded rock, and the shells of dead marine animals,
sink to the bottom of the sea, where they become crushed under
increasing layers and compressed into rocks   10 metals

Physical processes

Electricity and magnetism

Static charge

Examiner's tips and your notes

Do not use the word 'static' by itself. Use 'static charge' or 'static electricity'.

- **Conductors and insulators** – conductors allow electricity to flow through them, insulators do **not** allow electricity to flow through them.

- Metals are good conductors and most non-metals are not. Graphite – a form of carbon – is a non-metal which is a conductor.

- **Static electricity** – static means 'not moving'. Static electricity means electrical charge is not flowing.

An example of static charge is hair 'standing on end'.

- Plastic can be charged by friction, by rubbing it with cloth. The 'static electricity' on a charged plastic ruler can be used to attract small pieces of paper.

charged ruler

small pieces of paper

Remember this is the same as the poles of a magnet.

- **Charge**. There are two types of charge, **positive (+)** and **negative (−)**. Two simple rules to learn:

  1 **Unlike** charged materials attract and **like** (with the same charge) charged materials repel.

  2 **Charged** and **uncharged** materials will attract.

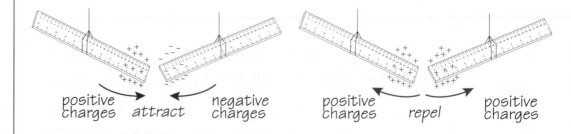

positive charges   attract   negative charges   positive charges   repel   positive charges

Currents in circuit

- A **circuit is a 'complete' path through which electric current can flow.**

- The circuit is usually made from conducting material such as copper wire (any metal could be used but copper is the best).

- For **electric current to flow, energy is needed**, usually a battery (cells) or a lab pack. These provide the **voltage** or **potential difference**.

  Voltage or p.d. is measured in volts.

- Current will **not** flow if there is a gap in a circuit.

- The circuit can be arranged in one of two ways; **series** or **parallel**.

Series and parallel circuits

- Trace your finger around the circuit from the energy source. If you can complete all the circuit without taking your finger off, and without touching the same line twice, it is in **series**.

- A **parallel** circuit has different routes available for the current to flow through (you cannot keep your finger on the paper).

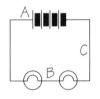

series circuit

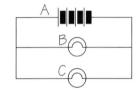

parallel circuit

Some important points to remember about the two types of circuit:

- If one of the bulbs in the series circuit 'blows' or is unscrewed, the other will also go out.

- If one of the bulbs in the parallel circuit 'blows' or is unscrewed the other will stay on.

- The way the circuit is connected, i.e. in series or in parallel, is very important when measuring the amount of current in a circuit.

- The current in a series circuit is the **same at each part of the circuit.**

- If the current at A in the series circuit above, is 1 A, then the current at B and C is also 1 A.

- The current in a parallel circuit is **not the same at all points of the circuit.** The current in the main circuit is the sum of the currents in the separate branches. If the current at B and C is 1 A, in the parallel circuit above, then the current at A is 2 A.

Measuring current

- Use an **ammeter**, connected in series in the circuit.

- Current is measured in **amperes** (amps for short, symbol is A).

- Current depends on the type of circuit (i.e. series or parallel), the number of cells (battery) in the circuit, and the number and type of any other component, i.e. the **resistance** of the circuit (the more components, the higher the resistance).

- The **resistance** of a circuit is how hard it is for the current to flow through it.

- Current is **not** used up as it flows round the circuit.

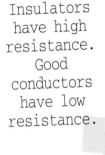

Resistance high, means current **low**; and resistance low, means current **high**.

Size of current

It is important to remember:

- Current is a **flow of charge**, the charge is negative particles (electrons).

- The **greater the number of cells, the higher the current**.

- The **lower the resistance** – e.g. the fewer bulbs in the circuit – the **greater the current**.

- The **thinner the wire**, the **higher the resistance** and the lower the current.

- The **thicker the wire**, the **lower the resistance** and the higher the current.

- The **longer the wire**, the **higher the resistance** and the lower the current.

- The **shorter the wire**, the **lower the resistance** and the higher the current.

Insulators have high resistance. Good conductors have low resistance.

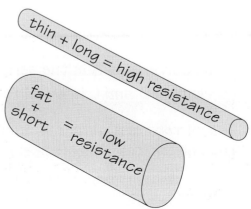

thin + long = high resistance

fat + short = low resistance

Circuit diagrams

Learn these circuit symbols.

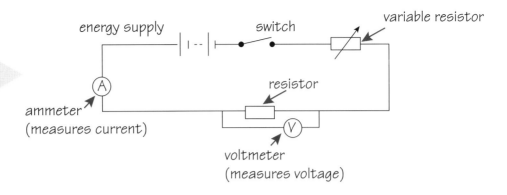

energy supply

switch

variable resistor

ammeter (measures current)

resistor

voltmeter (measures voltage)

Magnetic fields

Iron is magnetically soft, steel is magnetically hard.

- **Magnetic materials** – iron and steel are magnetic materials. Iron is easily magnetised and easily demagnetised. Steel is permanently magnetised. Most metals are not magnetic. All non-metals are **not** magnetic.

- **Fields** – **magnetic fields** are regions of space where magnetic materials 'experience' forces. An iron nail experiences a force in the 'field' of a magnet. The iron nail is attracted to the magnet. The field depends on the size and shape of the magnet.

Field patterns

Iron filings are often used to show simple field patterns.

- The field pattern around a bar magnet is as shown in the diagram below:

Notice the field direction arrows always point to **south** pole.

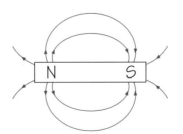

magnetic field

- **Poles** – the **north** pole of a bar magnet (the north seeking pole) points to magnetic north.

- The **south** pole of a bar magnet (south seeking pole) points to magnetic south.

• **Like** poles repel, **unlike** poles attract.

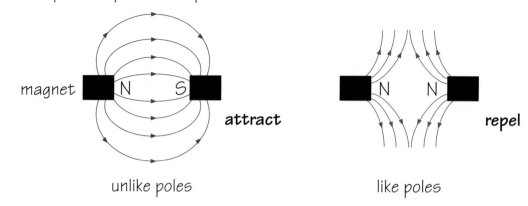

magnet

attract

repel

unlike poles

like poles

Electromagnets

• An electromagnet is usually made of soft iron, wrapped in wire through which a current passes.

• The field around a coil of wire with a current flowing through it is like a bar magnet.

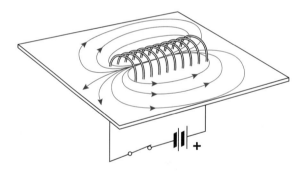

• Electromagnet can be switched on and off (as the current is switched on and off).

• An electromagnet has a north and south pole (just like a bar magnet).

• The poles of the magnet can be reversed by changing the direction of the current.

Easy to remember three 'Cs': Current, Coil, Core.

• Electromagnet can be made stronger by increasing the <u>**current**</u> (more batteries), putting more turns on the <u>**coil**</u>, and using a soft iron <u>**core**</u> (bigger nails).

Electromagnet devices

Electromagnets are used in everyday devices such as relays, electric bells, cranes and circuit breakers.

Electric bell

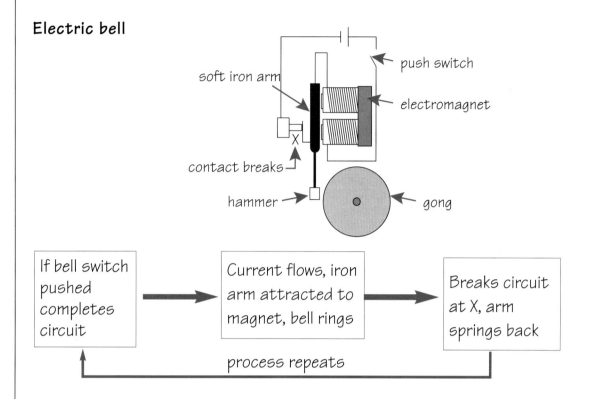

If bell switch pushed completes circuit	→	Current flows, iron arm attracted to magnet, bell rings	→	Breaks circuit at X, arm springs back

process repeats

Relay switch (electromagnetic switch)

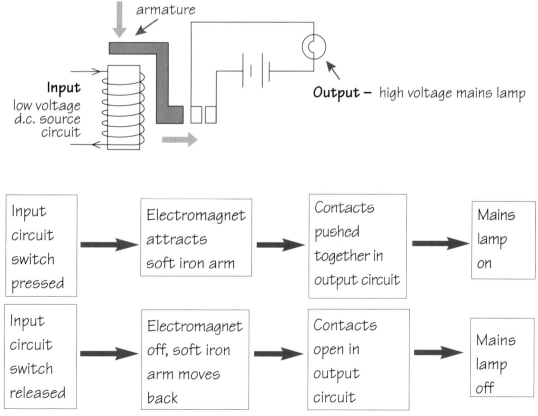

Input circuit switch pressed	→	Electromagnet attracts soft iron arm	→	Contacts pushed together in output circuit	→	Mains lamp on
Input circuit switch released	→	Electromagnet off, soft iron arm moves back	→	Contacts open in output circuit	→	Mains lamp off

Electricity and magnetism

Questions

1 What do we call a material which will allow current to flow through it? _____

2 Which of the following are electrical conductors: glass, copper, carbon, aluminium, rubber? _____

3 Which from the above list are insulators? _____

4 How can you charge a plastic rod? _____

5 Name the types of electrical charge. _____

6 Will materials with like charges attract or repel? _____

7 What do we use to measure current and in what unit is it measured? _____

8 What is used to measure voltage and in what unit is it measured? _____

9 What happens to the current when more cells are added to the circuit? _____

10 What happens to the current when the resistance of the circuit increases? _____

11 Name these circuit symbols.

(a) ⊸⊸ .... (b) ⊸⟍⊸ ....

(c) ⊣▭⊢ .... (d) ⊣⧄⊢ ....

(e) ⊣▭⊢ .... (f) ─◠─ ....

(g) ─Ⓥ─ .... (h) ─Ⓐ─ ....

(i) ─┤▮─ .... (j) ─┤▮┄▮─ ....

12 Name two magnetic materials. _____

13 Will **unlike** poles of a magnet attract or repel? _____

14 Name three ways of increasing the strength of an electromagnet. (a) _____ (b) _____ (c) _____

15 Name two devices which use an electromagnet. _____

Forces and motion

Examiner's tips and your notes

The unit of force is the **Newton**. A spring balance is made of a spring which stretches **evenly**, i.e. if it stretches 1 cm for 1 N it will stretch 2 cm for 2 N.

Forces and linear motion

Work is done when a force moves an object. The amount of work depends upon the distance:

$$W = F \times d \qquad\qquad \text{Units} = \text{Newton Metres} - \text{Nm}.$$

Convert mass to weight: kg x 10

Weight

- Weight is a force x acceleration of gravity. On Earth, weight = mass x g. For example, if your mass is 50 kg, your weight is 50 x 10 = 500 N (g = 10).

Speed

- To find out the speed of an object you need to know the distance travelled and the time taken to travel that distance.

$$\text{average speed (m/s)} = \frac{\text{distance travelled (m)}}{\text{time taken (s)}}$$

Use this to help.

- Sometimes we need to rearrange this equation to find out the time taken or the distance travelled:

Distance = speed x time	Time = distance/speed

Speed = distance/time

The speed of an object is measured in metres per second.

Balanced forces

- Forces act on moving objects. Forces which are balanced produce no change in the movement of an object. For example, the thrust (T) force of the car below is the same as the drag (D) force, so it will **stay still** (if not already moving) or continue to move at **constant speed**.

20 N ← → 20 N
  D   T

CONSTANT SPEED

or remains stationary

Unbalanced forces

- Forces which are not equal in size and direction will make an object speed up (accelerate) or slow down (decelerate) or change direction. If T is greater than D, the car above will accelerate.

Friction

- Frictional forces (e.g. air resistance) slow down a moving object. The effect of air resistance on a descending parachute means it does not descend faster and faster but reaches a constant speed (terminal velocity – final speed) when the forces are equal.

Parachutist reaches a terminal velocity when:
force up (air friction) = force down (gravity).

f and g are equal.

- **Friction always opposes the movement of an object and the faster the speed the greater the friction.** Friction causes heating and wearing away. This can be reduced by lubrication and streamlining.

- **Road safety** – The effect of friction between a tyre and the road is important for safety reasons. The time taken for a car to stop is called the total stopping distance.

thinking distance + braking distance = total stopping distance

- When it is wet and icy, frictional forces are reduced and braking distance is increased.

Forces and rotation

Turning forces

- Forces can be used to turn an object about a pivot — e.g. see-saw.

- The turning effect of a force is called a **moment (Nm)**.

moment of a force (Nm) = force (N) x perpendicular distance to pivot (m)

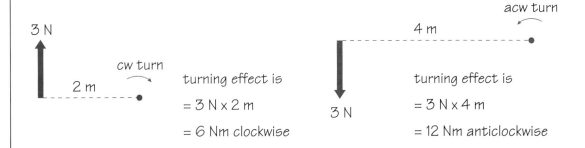

3 N

cw turn

2 m

turning effect is

= 3 N x 2 m

= 6 Nm clockwise

acw turn

4 m

3 N

turning effect is

= 3 N x 4 m

= 12 Nm anticlockwise

- Turning effect is greater if force is greater or distance is greater.

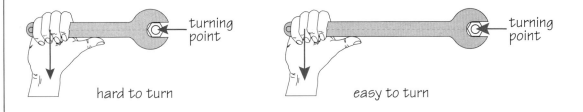

turning point

hard to turn

turning point

easy to turn

Law of moments: anticlockwise moments = clockwise moments

This see-saw is balanced because clockwise moment is 10 Nm and anticlockwise moment is 10 Nm.

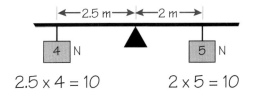

|←2.5 m→|←2 m→|

4 N   5 N

2.5 x 4 = 10   2 x 5 = 10

Force and pressure

Pressure

Calculate pressure using:

Use this to help.

$$\text{Pressure (N/m}^2) = \frac{\text{Force (N)}}{\text{Area (m}^2)}$$

This can be rearranged as:

Force = Pressure x Area	Area = Force/Pressure

Pressure is measured in Newtons per square metre, also called Pascal (Pa). It can also be measured in N/cm^2 if area is in cm^2.

- **Calculations** – A force of 10 N acts on an area of 5 cm^2. What is the pressure?
  10/5 = 2 N/cm^2.

  Small area = high pressure.

- A pressure of 5 Pa acts on an area of 5 m^2. What force is exerted? **5 x 5 = 25 N.**

- **Increasing pressure** – The pressure of an object increases if the area decreases – e.g. sharp blade of knife or high heel shoes.

  An elephant would do less damage if it trod on your toe than a lady in high heels, because the elephant's foot has a bigger area than a high heel.

Force on small area.

Example of high pressure

- **Decreasing pressure** – The pressure of an object decreases if the surface area increases – e.g. snow shoes or skis.

Force on large area.

Example of low pressure

Forces and motion

Questions

1 What unit do we measure force in? _____

2 Weight is a force. How is mass in Kg converted to weight in Newtons? _____

3 How can we calculate the speed of a moving object?

_____

4 An athlete runs 400 m in 60 seconds. What is the speed of the athlete? _____

5 Look at the diagram of a parachutist. He is travelling at a constant speed. What can we say about the forces F and W?

_____
_____
_____
_____

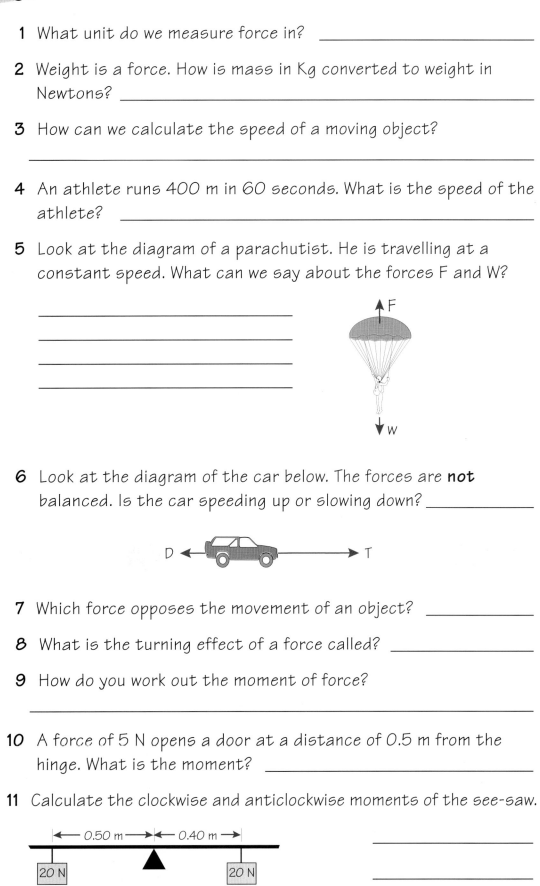

6 Look at the diagram of the car below. The forces are **not** balanced. Is the car speeding up or slowing down? _____

7 Which force opposes the movement of an object? _____

8 What is the turning effect of a force called? _____

9 How do you work out the moment of force?

_____

10 A force of 5 N opens a door at a distance of 0.5 m from the hinge. What is the moment? _____

11 Calculate the clockwise and anticlockwise moments of the see-saw.

_____

_____

Is it balanced? _____

12 How do you work out pressure ? _____

_____

13 Calculate the pressure exerted by a force of 20 N on an area of 0.1 m^2. _____

_____

14 Calculate the force acting on an area of 5 m^2 if the pressure is 5 Pa. _____

_____

15 The two boxes A and B have exactly the same weight. Which will have the highest pressure?

_____

_____

Light and sound

Behaviour of light

Compare
this to
sound –
only
330 m/s.

Light waves travel in straight lines at 300,000,000 m/s.

- It has a very short wavelength.

- The Sun, stars and bulbs give out light; they are luminous. Most objects reflect light (are non-luminous). This page reflects light into our eyes.

Shadows

- Shadows form because light travels in straight lines and is stopped by opaque (non-transparent) objects.

- Type of shadow depends on light:
  small light source = sharp shadow.
  large light source = blurred edges.

- Moon and Earth cast large shadows – **eclipses.**
  Sun – Moon – Earth 'day goes dark' – order of **solar** eclipse.
  Sun – Earth – Moon 'Moon goes dark' – order of **lunar** eclipse.

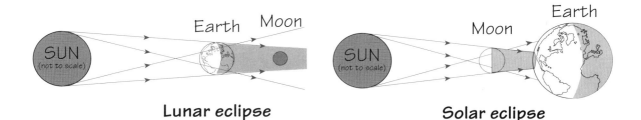

Lunar eclipse   **Solar eclipse**

Reflection

- When light hits a polished flat surface, it is reflected (it bounces back). It bounces back at the same angle as it hits the surface.

Make sure
you can draw
this and
name the
rays.

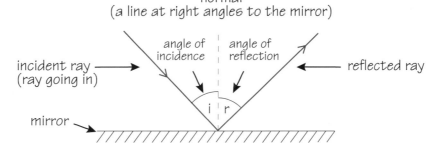

- **The law of reflection** – the angle of incidence (i) = the angle of reflection (r)
  $$i = r$$

You need to draw this diagram.

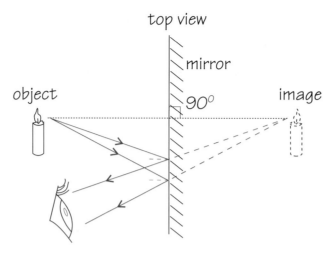

- Image in a flat mirror is:

    1. as far behind the mirror as the object is in front.
    2. **virtual** – no rays go through it (NOT REAL).
    3. the same size.
    4. laterally inverted (reversed side to side).

Refraction

- The **bending** of light as it **changes speed** as it crosses between **two different materials**.

    Light travels faster in air than in glass – the light ray bends as it goes into and out of the glass block.

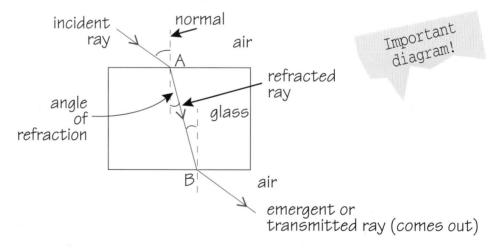

- A ray from air to glass is refracted (bent) towards the normal (slows down).

- A ray from glass to air is refracted (bent) away from the normal (speeds up).

- This has the effect of moving the ray sideways. Light striking the block at right angles goes straight through. This is the normal ray.

- Refraction occurs in other materials – water, perspex, etc.

Colour

Learn this diagram.

A prism splits white light into a spectrum:

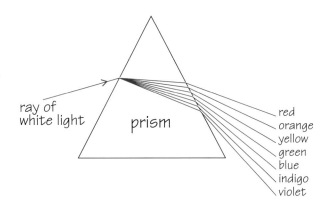

Red, Orange, Green, Yellow, Indigo, Blue, Violet.

ray of white light — prism — red / orange / yellow / green / blue / indigo / violet

- The seven colours can be remembered as **ROY G BIV**.

- Different wavelengths in white light give different colours; **violet** = short wavelength and is bent **the most**. **Red** is bent the least.

- **Primary colours** – red, green and blue – primary colours cannot be made from any other colours.

Learn how the secondary colours are made.

- **Secondary colours** – yellow, magenta and cyan.
  1. red and green = yellow
  2. red and blue = magenta
  3. blue and green = cyan

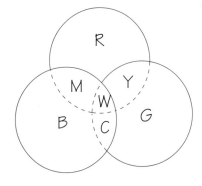

- **Filters** only allow certain wavelengths of light through – e.g. a red filter passes only red light and absorbs all others. A blue filter allows only blue light through.

- **Reflected colours** – The colour an object appears depends on the colour of the light it is seen in. In white light, a blue jumper looks blue – it absorbs all colours apart from blue, which it reflects. In red light, it looks black (there is no blue light to reflect back). In **red** light a red object looks **red**, in **white** light a red object looks **red** and in **blue** light a red object looks **black**.

Hearing

Three parts
to the ear:
outer,
middle,
inner.

- **Vibrations** produce sound. The vibration travels as a wave to the ear.

- **Outer** ear – vibrations cause the eardrum to vibrate.

- **Middle** ear – vibrations passed to three small bones.

- **Inner** ear – vibrations passed to liquid in the **cochlea**, stimulates nerves, sends messages via the auditory nerve to the brain.

Vibrations and sound waves

- Sound waves cannot travel through a vacuum (light waves can).

- Need a material – solid, liquid or gas – to pass through.

You cannot hear in space!

- The speed of light is approximately a million times faster than the speed of sound.

- The type of sound heard depends upon the **amplitude** and **frequency** of the vibration.

- A sound wave can be drawn as below:

a = amplitude

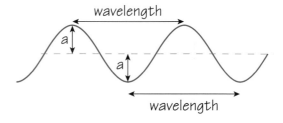

Amplitude

- How 'loud' a sound is depends upon its amplitude.

- The **bigger the amplitude,** the **louder** the sound (the bigger the wave).

- Our ears can be damaged very easily by loud sounds. Very loud sounds (explosives, etc.) may damage the eardrum and the bones of the middle ear.

- Persistent loud noise – such as from personal stereos – may cause permanent damage to the cochlea, resulting in deafness.

Pitch and frequency

- The '**pitch**' of a note, i.e. whether it is high or low, depends upon the frequency. Frequency is the number of vibrations per second.

high   low

Frequency is measured in Hertz (Hz).

- Greater the number of vibrations, higher the frequency, higher the pitch.

- The range of frequencies we can hear varies with age. The usual range is 20 Hz (Hertz) to 20,000 Hz. Many animals have a greater range – e.g. bats, dolphins. Above 20,000 Hz is called ultrasound.

Ultrasound is used in medicine for pre-natal scanning.

Light and sound

Questions

1 What do we call objects that are sources of light? _____

2 Which is faster – the speed of light or sound? _____

3 What is the law of reflection?_____

4 Describe the image seen in a flat mirror.

(a) _____

(b) _____

(c) _____

5 What is the bending of light called? _____

6 The diagram below shows a light ray passing from air to glass. Which ray is:

incident?   _____

refracted?   _____

reflected?   _____

transmitted?_____

7 A prism disperses white light into a spectrum. Name the colours of the spectrum. _____

8 What are the primary colours? _____ _____ _____

9 What are the secondary colours? _____ _____ _____

10 What causes a sound wave? _____

11 What determines the 'loudness' of sound? _____

12 What determines the 'pitch' of sound?_____

13 Which of the waves below will be the loudest? _____

14 Which of the waves above will have the lowest pitch? _____

15 Can sound travel through a vacuum?_____

Energy resources and energy transfer

Resources

- Energy resources include oil, coal, gas (fossil fuels), food, wind, moving water, batteries, etc. Some are renewable (will not run out) and some are non-renewable. **The Sun** is the source of most energy resources – e.g. food is 'trapped chemical energy' made by photosynthesis, using **sunlight**.

- Exceptions to the above – e.g. tidal energy due to gravitational pull of moon.

Renewable and non-renewable resources

renewable	non-renewable
solar, wind, waves	coal, oil, gas
biomass, hydroelectric power	nuclear
tidal, geothermal	

Advantages and disadvantages to all of the above:

- non-renewable – lots of cheap energy available but very bad for the environment – lots of pollution produced – adds to greenhouse effect (fossil fuels) – will run out eventually.

- renewable – free and environmentally friendly (usually) but not much energy produced – expensive to set up – not always available (not always sunny/windy, etc.)

Electrical energy

- Electrical energy is widely used and is generated from many of the energy resources above. In non-renewable power stations the fuel is used to heat water to make steam to drive the turbines.

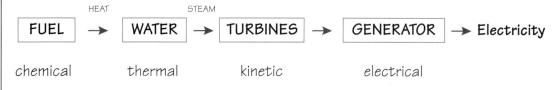

In renewable power stations, the fuel is used to drive the turbines directly – no need for a boiler.

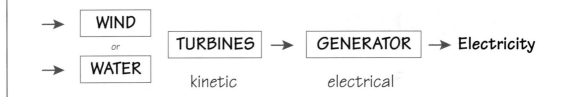

Solar cells produce electricity directly, by using sunlight to excite electrons – very expensive!

Conservation

Energy types

Catapults store 'elastic' potential and high objects store 'gravitational' potential.

- Energy is measured in Joules (J).

- Forms of energy include heat, light, sound, electrical, chemical, potential (elastic and gravitational), kinetic (movement) and nuclear.

- Energy is useful when it is changed from one form to another – **work** is done.

In a battery **chemical** energy is transformed into useful **electrical** energy.

An iron changes **electrical** energy into **heat** energy.

Energy transfer

When energy is transferred it is conserved, i.e. it is **not** used up.

This means if you start with 100J of energy you end up with a 100J. This is important – **the conservation of energy**.

- The energy resulting from a transfer is not always useful – it may be dissipated. This means it cannot be used as a resource. We say it is **wasted**. This 'waste' energy is often transferred to heat energy (but not always). A torch converts chemical energy (in battery) to electrical energy, to light energy (in bulb). However the bulb gets warm so some energy is wasted as heat. The heat energy lost from the bulb is not useful.

Heat energy

- The temperature of an object is measured with a thermometer in degrees Celsius.

- The unit of heat energy is the **Joule**.

A large warm object has more heat energy than a small hot one.

- The temperature of an object is not the same as the total heat energy contained within it. Compare a teaspoon of 'boiling' water and a bath full of 'warm' water. The spoonful has a higher temperature, but the bath has greater total energy because it has many more molecules.

- When you heat an object, you give the molecules more **kinetic** energy, raising its temperature.

- Heat energy is transferred from **hot** to **cold** objects.

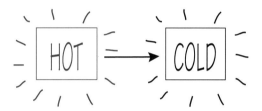

Remember – heat passes from the hotter to the cooler object.

Energy resources and energy transfer

Questions

1 What unit is used to measure energy? _____

2 Name a renewable source of energy. _____

3 Name a non-renewable source of energy. _____

4 What is the main type of energy produced by a car?

_____

5 What is the main type of energy produced by a radio?

_____

6 What type of energy is stored in a battery? _____

7 What type of energy is produced by a battery? _____

8 What type of energy is stored in a spring in a clockwork toy?

_____

9 What is the main source of energy for the Earth?

_____

10 What is the source of energy in hydroelectric power stations?

_____

11 Many energy conversions include some 'wasted' form of energy.
    What is a common form of waste energy? _____

12 Which type of energy is also known as thermal energy?

_____

13 What are the main energy conversions in a renewable power
    station? _____

14 What do you measure temperature with, and in what unit?

_____

15 Describe the difference between temperature and heat energy.

_____

_____

_____

The Earth and beyond

The Earth

- The time it takes for the Earth to complete 1 spin is called 1 day. As the Earth spins, one side is facing the Sun. This is day. For the opposite side, it is night.

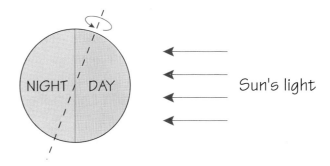

- The spin of the Earth causes the daily changes in the position of the Sun and other stars. **This is very important**.

- The Sun rises in the **east** and sets in the **west**. At noon it is directly overhead in the **south**.

- Earth's axis is tilted, therefore at certain times of the year we are either closer to or further away from the Sun. This explains why we have seasons of the year.

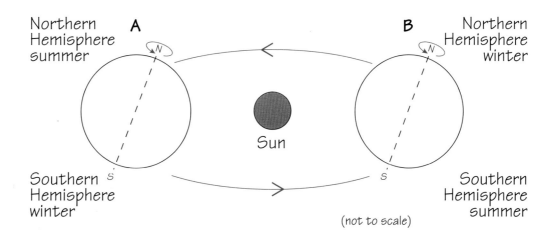

- The time it takes for the Earth to orbit (go around) the Sun is 1 Year (365¼ days).

Satellites

- The moon is a natural satellite of the Earth, i.e. it orbits the Earth trapped by the Earth's gravity. It does **not** give out its own light. It reflects light from the Sun.

- It orbits the Earth once every 27–28 days. It also spins on its axis every 27–28 days.

- Artificial satellites sent into orbit around the Earth can be used to observe the Earth and space, or for communication purposes.

- Gravity keeps satellites in orbit. If the pull of gravity and the speed of the satellite are balanced, the satellite stays in orbit.
  If speed too slow – falls back to earth.
  If speed too fast – spins off into space.

The Solar System

- It consists of the Sun (our star), planets, moons and asteroid belt.

- The nine planets orbit the Sun in slightly squashed circles (ellipses) and are kept in position by the massive pull of the Sun's gravity.

- The Sun is massive compared to the planets.

- The planets vary in size and distance from the Sun and therefore have vastly different conditions on their surfaces.

- Pluto's orbit is at a different angle from the other planets.

In general, the greater the distance from the Sun the colder the temperature.

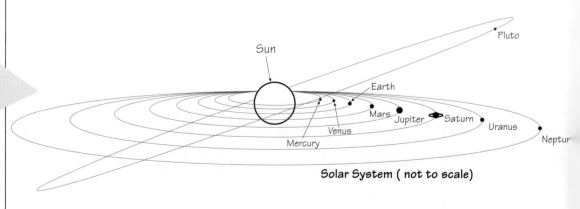

Solar System (not to scale)

Think of a
sentence to
help you
with the
planet
names.

- Planets are Mercury, Venus, Earth, Mars, Jupiter, Saturn, Uranus, Neptune and Pluto (Mercury being the closest to the Sun).

- The four inner planets are relatively small and rocky, volcanic in nature. The outer planets are giant balls of gas (not Pluto).

- The planets nearer to the Sun travel more quickly, therefore have shorter years. The length of year varies with distance from the Sun.

- A year is the length of time taken for the planet to orbit the Sun.

- Planets do not give out their own light, they reflect the Sun's light.

- Planets appear to move across the background of stars in a night sky because they are much nearer to us than the stars.

- The Sun, the star in our Solar System, stays in a fixed star pattern in the sky. Star patterns can be identified and are called constellations.

- The Sun is one of millions of stars in our galaxy.

- Our galaxy is one of millions in the universe.

- The distance between planets is tiny compared to the distance between stars. The distance between stars is tiny compared to the distance between galaxies.

The Earth and beyond

Questions

1 Name the nine planets in the Solar System in order, starting with the planet nearest the Sun.

_____ _____ _____

_____ _____ _____

_____ _____ _____

2 Describe the motion of the Earth. _____

_____

3 What force determines the movement of the planets around the Sun? _____

4 How can we see other planets? _____

5 What is a satellite? _____

6 What can an artificial satellite be used for? _____

Physical processes • Answers

Electricity and magnetism

1 conductor   2 copper, carbon, aluminium   3 glass, rubber
4 by rubbing (friction)   5 positive and negative   6 repel
7 ammeter – Amps   8 voltmeter – Volts   9 current increases
10 current decreases   11 a) closed switch b) open switch
c) fuse d) variable resistor e) resistor f) bulb g) voltmeter
h) ammeter i) cell j) battery   12 iron, steel   13 attract
14 a) increasing current (more batteries) b) increasing number of
turns on coil c) use of bigger soft iron core   15 any two from: bell,
relay, loudspeaker, circuit-breaker

Forces and motion

1 Newtons   2 multiply kg x 10 (10 N/kg)   3 speed = distance/
time   4 speed: 400/60 = 6.67 m/s   5 equal
6 speeding up   7 friction   8 moment   9 moment = force x
distance from pivot   10 moment: 5 x 0.5 = 2.5 Nm
11 clockwise = 10 Nm, anticlockwise = 10 Nm, yes
12 pressure = force/area   13 pressure: 20/0.1 = 200 Nm^2
14 force: 5 x 5 = 25 N   15 B

Light and sound

1 luminous   2 light   3 angle of incidence equals angle of
reflection   4 virtual image distance equals object distance / image
is same size as object   5 refraction   6 incident = C,
refracted = B, reflected = D, transmitted = A   7 red, orange,
yellow, green, blue, indigo, violet   8 red, green, blue
9 yellow, cyan, magenta   10 vibration   11 amplitude
12 frequency   13 B   14 C   15 no

Energy resources and energy transfer

1 Joule   2 any from: wind, tidal, solar, wood, geothermal, moving water   3 any from: coal, oil, gas, nuclear fuel   4 kinetic
5 sound   6 chemical   7 electrical   8 potential (elastic)
9 Sun   10 water (potential)   11 heat   12 heat
13 kinetic/electrical   14 thermometer – Celsius
15 temperature is a measure of 'hotness'. Heat energy is a measure of internal energy. A warm large object will have more total energy than a small hotter object because it will have many more molecules.

The Earth and beyond

1 Mercury, Venus, Earth, Mars, Jupiter, Saturn, Uranus, Neptune, Pluto   2 spins on its axis, orbits the Sun in nearly circular orbit.
3 gravity   4 reflected light from the Sun   5 a body which orbits (goes round) another.   6 communication, weather, monitoring (spy)